SCARLETS

THE OFFICIAL HISTORY
BY ALUN GIBBARD

GRAFFEG

Scarlets The Official History published
by Graffeg September 2015 © Copyright
Graffeg 2015 ISBN 9781909823730

Scarlets The Official History
Text © Alun Gibbard

Designed and produced by Graffeg
www.graffeg.com

Graffeg Limited, 24 Stradey Park
Business Centre, Mwrwg Road,
Llangennech, Llanelli, Carmarthenshire
SA14 8YP Wales UK
Tel 01554 824000 www.graffeg.com

Graffeg are hereby identified as the
authors of this work in accordance with
section 77 of the Copyrights, Designs and
Patents Act 1988.

A CIP Catalogue record for this book is
available from the British Library.

SCARLETS

THE OFFICIAL HISTORY
BY ALUN GIBBARD

SCARLETS

GRAFFEG

Contents

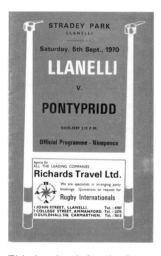

This is a book for the fan, both of Llanelli Rugby Club and, more generally, of the wonderful sport of Rugby Union. Inspired by some of the rich stories and legendary players associated with the club, this is not a book crammed with stats, team lists and committee minutes. Instead this book brings together the highlights of each period of the club's history, as it reflects upon the club and its relationship with the town and its supporters over the last hundred and forty years.

What was Llanelli like in the days before the club formed? This is the context from which the club grew, the social fabric that gave it its being. The club's links to heavy industry are established here, the foundation for the game as being of the working man.

The story of John Rogers, the Rugby public school boy who came to Llanelli to manage some of the town's foundries. He brought the game with him and set about forming a team, which quickly became a club. The early days and early stars of the club outlined, including the first victory against Australia.

The song that has become the club's anthem, linked to that victory against Australia by the addition of the 'Who Beat the Wallabies?' verse. But where did the song come from? What's the story of the popular song and how did it become Llanelli's own?

42 The Era of Giants 1918-1939

The rugby lull during the war years is over and a period that was a golden era for the club begins. The 1920s are referred to as The Era of Giants in the club's history, with many stars putting on the famous jersey, including the legendary Albert Jenkins.

50 Stradey Park

The cathedral of Scarlets rugby for nearly a hunded years. But how did the club end up playing there? The major period of redevelopment at the ground was in the 1950s, when it became a leading rugby stadium. But when did it close, and why?

64 The Magnificent Seven and a Fistful of Stars 1945-1959

An era for new heroes. Seven Scarlets were chosen to play for Wales in 1946-1947 and by the time the new Stradey had taken shape there were new heroes again in the shape of R. H. Williams and colleagues.

72 Moscow — Men of Steel go behind the Iron Curtain

In 1957 Llanelli Rugby Club made an unusual journey – behind the Iron Curtain to Moscow. They took part in the World Youth Games, the only rugby club from the United Kingdom to be invited. For some games, Llanelli were on the scoreboard as Wales. Find out how they got to the final and the trials and tribulations of their journey there and back.

80 The Stradey Swinging Sixties: 1960-1969

An era of change in Stradey, which saw the seeds sown for the golden era that followed in the next decade. Future stars such as Delme Thomas, Phil Bennett and Derek Quinnell pulled on the Scarlet jersey for the first time as did Barry John. There were changes off the pitch as well, both in the board room and in the town, as the grip of traditional heavy industry started to loosen.

88 Oh no, we don't want coaches!

The biggest change of all was the introduction of coaches to the game, thus ending the captain's role as the man in charge of training. Ieuan Evans came first, followed by the Maestro Carwyn James. But not everyone welcomed this new innovation.

92 All Blacks, Cups and Carwyn 1970–1979

Another golden era which saw success after success. The game against South Africa in 1970 kicked it all off. Even though they lost, the team went on to beat the All Blacks, win four cup finals in a row, and supply Wales with many new internationals. And of course, Llanelli's Carwyn James coached the Lions to a series win in New Zealand.

108 Who Beat the All Blacks?

Their finest hour! The day the All Blacks were felled and Llanelli pubs ran dry. Players recall their memories of this day – players who were then, of course, men with day jobs, with many back in work the day after their triumph. Find out what Gareth Jenkins did with a £10 note, while others record the impact the game had far beyond the edges of the Loughor Bridge.

118 Rebuilding to be the Best in Britain 1980–1994

These were somewhat leaner years for the club, but nevertheless they brought moments of great success. The era culminated in the massive achievement of the team beating Australia, winning the league and being voted the best club in Britain. It was a fitting climax to what was to be the end of the amateur era in rugby as the age of professionalism dawned.

128 Many came, many saw, many were conquered!

Llanelli has welcomed teams from all over the world since early on in its history. That tradition has come to an end in the professional era, and this chapter is of historical value in that it chronicles a part of Llanelli rugby history that won't happen again. The major games against Southern Hemisphere clubs are recounted, and we learn of other teams who have played against Llanelli from around the world.

142 New home, new name, same heritage 1995-2015

The years of the professional era, as players became paid athletes for the first time. European cup rugby began and the days of regionalism dawned. The Scarlets succeeded in securing stand-alone status as a region, representing the west and the north as well as being seen as the club of Welsh speaking Wales. No one embodied all of this more vividly than the legendary Grav. His funeral in Stradey was a truly unique event.

172 Parc y Scarlets

Despite the heart-felt nostalgia and the deep-rooted loyalty, Stradey had to close and a brand new stadium opened. Unbeknown to the club, the new site was the location of a stadium that stood on the same place a hundred years earlier. Parc y Scarlets is the only new, purpose built club stadium in the UK.

188 Internationals and Lions

A list of all Scarlets who've played for their countries – Wales and others – and a list of British and Irish Lions from the club.

LLANELLY IN 1821.

Presented to the readers of the "Llanelly and County Guardian," Jan. 3rd, 1907.

Welshmen are proud of the artist David Cox, who flourished at the beginning of last century, and it is to be regretted that we have no nearer association with him than Kidwelly. But Cox's friend, companion, and fellow-artist, Parry, is connected with a Llanelly family, and it is this Mr. Parry who, about 1821, painted the original of the picture reproduced above. The point of view is the flank of the Bigyn, not far from where the County School now stands. Commencing on the left hand of the spectator are Llanelly Flats, where small craft lay on the sands to discharge or load their cargoes before the Carmarthenshire Docks provided better facilities. Next appear the Erw, Vauxhall, and Spring Gardens. Then we have the Old Church, with its spire of long ago, and its tower of to-day. It is partially eclipsed by Llanelly House or Mansion. On the extreme right are two lines of houses—the upper is Mount Pleasant, the lower the Swansea Road. In the distance is outlined Old Stradey House, at the foot of Pembrey mountain. This old house appears very near the sea, and was so until the making of the (now) Great Western Railway kept the tide from coming any longer almost up to Cille, and well to the North of the now Pembrey Road. The battered and faded original of our picture—a water-colour on paper mounted on canvas is in the possession of Mr. C. E. A. Jones, of Cilymaenllwyd, a grandson of the artist; and there is a copy in oils on the walls of the Free Library.

From 1852 to 1854, Mrs. Havard, the wife of a Wesleyan minister, stationed at Llanelly, produced quite a number of pictures, in pencil and colour, of the town and neighbourhood as they then were. These pictures possess great historical interest, and the one we reproduce depicts the very heart of our old town, grouped as it was around the Parish Church as a centre. The original was made for the late Mr. James Buckley, and is here copied by the kind permission of Mrs. W. J. Buckley. John Wesley has, more than once, walked down Church-street, on the extreme left of the spectator, to preach to a crowd which would occupy the space in the foreground. That space was, and had long been, the Market Place, and we see's cookings, shoes, and earthenware displayed for sale. The second named wares still give a nickname—"Heol yr Esgidian," to part of Church-street. On our right of the ancient Lych Gate, and almost immediately under two printed notices on the walk, is the prone figure of a man in the stocks. Young Mr. James Buckley on horseback talks to Squire Chambers and his wife; the Misses Hall, carrying bell-shaped parasols, have their backs to us; a little nearer Davy Thomas, the view, stands, tall in land; and old Moses, the Jew pedlar, faces the beholder. This tall trees on our right, are in front of the old Pemberton Mansion House, where the Athenæum now stands. At the time of the picture, the house was the residence of Dr. Cook below, and the infant Chamber of Commerce was cradled in the upper storey. Further back stands Llanelly House, home of many generations of Stepneys, but then occupied by Mr. William Chambers and his family.

Foreword

It was an honour and a privilege to be invited to write a foreword for a book that will mean so much to so many people.

Scarlets is a club and a brand known the world over, and now a region that is held in the highest regard by people from all walks of life.

My own association with the club goes back some five years and the proud history belonging to this place is something that we're all aware of and appreciate.

I have however always believed that we need more confidence in our ability to develop indigenous talent while confirming our status as a community club through democratising it even further.

Barcelona, in recent years, have regularly fielded players that were developed through their own academy and there is no reason why this club shouldn't have the same philosophy. Over the last few years we have put in place a number of initiatives that range from the grass roots to board level.

One grass roots initiative in support of all clubs in the region and the junior sections within those clubs allows free entry to Scarlets games for card carrying juniors, along with their coaches, team managers and referees. This is an initiative I am extremely proud of. It's our way of saying thank you to the junior game, which is critical to the future of the game here and in Wales.

Mine is a long-term vision that may provide the basis for future success. If I leave the club with a sustainable funding model and a loyal group of funding directors, ambassadors and supporters my time here will have been a success. It's not easy to achieve in any club but I think with the Scarlets, where we have such a strong community base and a great heritage, the model can work.

This book shows how strong that community base is in West Wales and we look forward to building on our great heritage and fanbase for the future.

Nigel Short
Chairman of the Scarlets board
September 2015

Above: Scarlets Chairman Nigel Short (left), with international opera star Bryn Terfel and Scarlets board member, Robert Williams.
Left: In the days before rugby and heavy industry, Llanelli was a quiet hamlet.

The Most Famous Rugby Club in the World

September 1970. That's when my own personal Scarlets history began. The Scarlets were playing against Pontypridd – I've still got the programme. My father took me, securing my place in a tradition that's nearly a century and a half old of fathers taking their sons, hand in hand, to see their first rugby game. I can't remember any details at all about the day, but I know I was there. A bit like the day I was born really.

I've followed the team ever since and seen many highs and many lows. I've been soaking wet on the Tanner Bank on a dark Wednesday evening; travelled on the coach to away games; invaded the pitch in '72; shared cup delights many times over; groaned, shouted and moaned, shoulder to shoulder with the army of Scarlets fans. What a delight therefore to be asked to write the story of Llanelli rugby club.

But it's a very responsible delight, as I knew this was to be the story of rugby royalty; a high profile club known the world over. It was also a responsible delight because whatever I wrote would be analysed and scrutinised as much as any performance by any referee over the last hundred years. We all have our own version of the history of Llanelli rugby club.

But the work is done, and contained within these pages are the many milestones on the long rugby road in Llanelli.

There are also challenges, other than the ones already mentioned, to writing such a history. For a start, it splits into two. The part that no-one alive remembers and the part that falls within living memory. Writing about both periods is tricky as the first means relying on documents only while the second can be influenced by people's memory. Both can be a bit unreliable for different reasons. The line between one period and the other is always changing, of course, as the older Scarlets fans leave us for the stadium in the sky, bringing the memory line ever closer to us. Trawling through both sources, and many more, has led to the work you are about to read.

The story of rugby in Llanelli. The story of how town and game grew up together. It's a story for the fan, the follower, the supporter. It's the story of the rugby club that's the most famous rugby club in the world.

Alun Gibbard

STRADEY PARK
LLANELLI

Saturday, 5th Sept., 1970

LLANELLI

V.

PONTYPRIDD

KICK-OFF 3.15 P.M.

Official Programme - Ninepence

Llanelli in the 1870s
A public school game in working class furnaces

Llanelli stood shoulder to sweaty shoulder with other towns along the South Wales coastline as heavy industry shaped the Wales of the time.

They were exciting times. Llanelli was a busy, bustling, growing place in the last decades of the nineteenth century. The number of people living in the town increased significantly as each decade gave way to the next, more than tripling from the beginning of the century to its end. At the beginning of the nineteenth century there were less people living in Llanelli than the number of Scarlets fans who would travel to an away game in Italy today.

Rolling fields reached down and touched the streets of the town centre, which couldn't even be called a town then. Sheep were a common sight, as occasional strollers and shoppers looked up to the hills from the not-so-busy, roughly structured, primitive streets. But before that century reached the promised 'three score years and ten' a rural village had changed into an industrial force and Llanelli had become a definite place to be towards the end of Victoria's days on the throne.

Llanelli stood shoulder to sweaty shoulder with other towns along the South Wales coastline as heavy industry shaped the Wales of the time. Coal, steel, iron, tin, lead, copper all formed part of the bubbling crucible that was industrial South Wales and Llanelli played its part as Victoria's reign progressed. As the nineteenth century drew to a close however, coal was no longer king in the Llanelli area. Neither was the town's shipping industry the power it had once been. The great Isambard Kingdom Brunel himself declared that 'Nature has not done much to fit Llanelly for a port.' (It was Llanelli with a 'y' then, it didn't change to an 'i' until the days of The Beatles.)

The ships hadn't gone completely, neither had the coal, but they weren't the force they had once been in Llanelli town and the cluster of villages that surrounded it. Llanelli was having

Left: New work, new workforce, new structures.

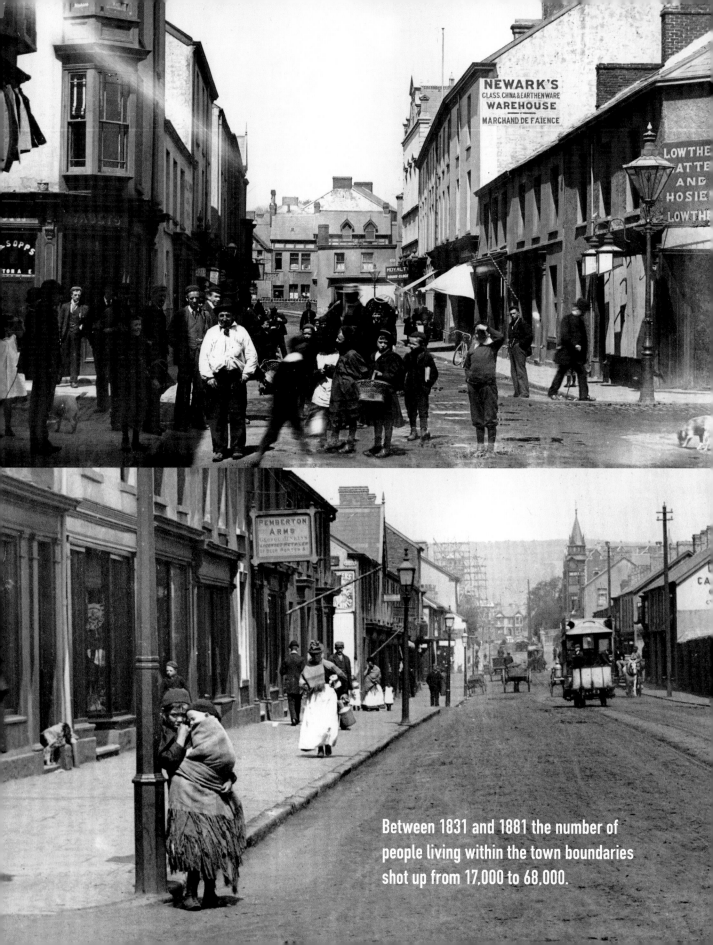

Between 1831 and 1881 the number of people living within the town boundaries shot up from 17,000 to 68,000.

to move on from being a town of colliers and sailors.

Instead, Llanelli made its mark on the industrial world primarily through tinplate. Seven tinplate factories were established in the town at the end of the nineteenth century. That's a lot of tin and a lot of work for a lot of people. They were established by moneyed gentlemen from outside the area, the industrial entrepreneurs who were bank-rolling and pioneering the industrial surge of the time.

Steelworks were started too by the same kind of gentleman. Tin works needed iron forges and foundries and they all depended on each other. Each area of the town had some form of industrial building that turned the wheels of heavy industry in Llanelli.

With all this activity, no town could stay the same. Between 1831 and 1881 the number of people living within the town boundaries shot

Left and top: Industry brought the prosperity of shops and Market Street, Station Road and Stepney Street flourished.
Above: Men of steel.

'Such a rapid growth in population in such dangerous and new heavy industries was sure to lead to illness and injury'

Above: Men who worked hard needed to play hard.
Page 17: Hotels and pubs welcomed workers and visitors alike. This one stood on the corner of Market Street and Park Street.

up from 17,000 to 68,000.That's a lot of people to find houses for, open shops for, build railways for and find things to do with their recreation time. The concept of leisure might not have been then what it is today, but they still needed things to do when the work and the chores were done.

This meant, for one thing, chapel on Sundays. Looking around the town today, the buildings where factory workers and owners alike could worship together still stand tall as a testament to the pride they put into their Sundays. They are architectural gems whether you believe or not, stone symbols of a town's expansion. An event at one of these chapels, Tabernacl, next to the Town Hall, saw a crowd of more than 1500 people gather to witness the laying of a memorial stone. The sheer magnitude of these buildings shows clearly how many people it would take to fill them. And they were full. Regularly.

However, to avoid giving the impression that industrial Llanelli was a little heaven on earth where everyone went to chapel, the town also had 125 pubs at the end of the nineteenth century. No doubt they too were full. Regularly. Today much is made of micro-breweries brewing their own. But there's nothing new under the sun as those pubs a hundred and fifty years ago testify – they too brewed their own. The hot foundries made for thirsty men and their unquenchable thirsts had to be met. One factory owner recognised this and set about doing something about it. He thought it would be better to build one brewery to supply many pubs, with the added bonus that his workers could slake the thirsts they built up in his factories in his pub as well. The result? Felinfoel Brewery which still brews and is still run by one of the same families who set it up.

The town already had another brewery, Buckley's. It had been in the town for a long, long time and has the quirky characteristic of being founded by a Methodist minister. The Reverend James' face can be seen on bottled beer to this day, even though his surname is no longer associated with brewing in the area.

Another liquid was also very much at a premium in a hot foundry town. Water was vital, not only to cool and wash the dirty workers but also to keep the foundries cool and stop them exploding! The Trebeddrod reservoir in the appropriately named village of Furnace was soon insufficient to meet all the town's needs. However, it took nearly ten years of planning, permission seeking and building before the Cwm Lliedi reservoir opened in 1878, holding 160 million gallons of water. A second resevoir was opened in 1903, this one holding 200 million gallons of water. The area where this is sited has now become rather fancifully known as Swiss Valley.

Such a rapid growth in population in such dangerous and new heavy industries was sure to lead to illness and injury, and somewhere was needed to deal with this. Three houses close together at the top of Bigyn Hill were leased and a hospital was opened.

The need for water and ale, and the needs of the soul, were being catered for in an ever-expanding town. Houses were being built everywhere, and pretty soon there was a clear distinction between the types of houses lived in by the well-off and the less well-off. The mushrooming working class yielded the new middle class, and both were somewhere below the factory owners and managers. However, they all had one other need in common. They worked hard... and they needed to play hard.

The oldest sporting club in the town is... well actually no, not that one. It's actually the cricket club where the townsfolk had been putting on their whites as far back as 1839. It was set up by a man from one of the famous families of Llanelli, William Chambers Jr. – the Chambers' giving the boxing world The Queensbury Rules that still guide pugilists in their sport to this day. They didn't play many far away teams in those days, as 'far away' was a lot further and a lot harder to get to than it is today. It would have taken three hours to get to Carmarthen, for example. So local teams were formed in each village, and the competition was both local and fierce; well, as fierce as cricket gets anyway!

Left: The smoke of industry dominated life outside the foundry too.

Right (top): Linking the West with the rest. Right (bottom): Signs of another booming pastime – a cycle shop.

So, as the 1870s loom, the town is establishing itself; it's coming of age and is most definitely a player on the world's industrial stage. Physically and communally the town was organising itself and things were happening in all areas of life. In this great age of development and invention throughout the UK new things were being built, opened and developed in Llanelli too.

In fact growth continued right up to the end of the century and beyond. A tramway system was installed, as was a telephone exchange. A post office was built in Cowell Street, a new market hall was built and, a little later, a glass and steel pavilion added to it which was somehow reminiscent of the vast railway terminuses of London. But perhaps the biggest change was still to come as, not long after the new century began, a new steelworks was built that would dominate the town for nearly a century. The Llanelli Steelworks was massive. It stretched along the coastline from Sandy to Pwll and employed thousands of men. It was soon nicknamed, 'The Klondike', a name that captured the hope local people clearly placed in this leviathan of a factory. This would bring new jobs and new wealth to the town and, indeed, the Klondike was to play a central role in the life of the rugby club. But before that could happen the rugby club needed to be formed, a club that one day would be known the world over.

The formation of Llanelli Rugby Club wasn't the result of a random collection of men walking out on to an empty field and playing a new game for the sake of it. The men you will shortly meet walked out from a definite social and cultural context and were brought together by the same set of circumstances as were guiding and shaping the town as a whole. They shared the same desire to play this new game and to start a new club at this particular moment in time. They probably weren't consciously aware of these influences, but they were definitely there as we look back from our advantageous viewpoint many years hence. The formation of Llanelli Rugby Club came about at a definite period in the history of the town. Rugby might be seen as a public school game in its origins, but as soon as it hit Llanelli, it took root in a town of workers who were creating a new town, and forming a rugby club was just one part of that bigger picture.

Beginnings are important. They set the tone, the spirit of what's to come. The foundations were laid that would set the path for Llanelli Rugby Club for the century that was to follow. These beginnings set the values that would guide the club through each warp and weft that lay ahead, no less so than on that famous day in 1972 when the mighty All Blacks were felled. But all that's still to come. For now, we need to turn to the very start, the story of how Llanelli Rugby Club was formed.

A Rugby Club is Born
1872-1914

The names Morewood and Rogers don't instantly spring to mind when thinking of the story of rugby in Llanelli. They probably don't spring to mind when considering the story of the town as a whole. But these two men played a leading part in the development of heavy industry in the town and in forming the rugby club. So who were they?

One of the many foundries and factories that opened in Llanelli in the last few decades of Queen Victoria's reign was the Marsh Iron Works, later the Marshfield Works then the Western Tinplate Works. The Marshfield Tap, a pub that has only very recently closed in the town, owes its name to this establishment. The Works was opened by Morewood and Rogers when they came to Llanelli at the beginning of the 1870s. They were very busy industrialists, they had already been in America opening factories and developing techniques to galvanise tinned iron. The fact they then came to Llanelli to ply their trade shows what kind of attraction the town held for those wanting to invest in, and develop heavy industry. In Llanelli, they went on to open The South Wales Works in Machynys, the Yspitty Tinplate Works in Bynea and two other factories in Baglan and Swansea.

But then tragedy struck when J. H. Rogers died. His wife, keen to secure her son's future and give him the stability he had lost through the passing of his father, asked Morewood if he could find employment for him in his Llanelli

works. At that time, Morewood was the most successful tinplate works owner in Britain. He lived in a very big house in Llangennech, on the outskirts of the town, where, in 1872, John D. Rogers, the son, went to live with him and started to work for his father's former business partner.

Between 1863 and 1866 John Rogers had been to Rugby Public School where he had played a ball game named after the school. When he moved to live and work in Llanelli, he brought that game with him and quickly set about introducing it to his new friends and workmates. The year he moved to Llangennech there are records of him taking a rugby ball to People's Park and having a kick about there. Today, this park stands behind the magnificent Town Hall, but in 1872 there was no town hall there and the fields were wide and open.

From that simple spontaneous recreational activity of some working men, Llanelli Rugby Club was born. The men of the town caught on instantly and there were plenty more kick abouts and informal rugby sessions. Soon, a group of men were gathered together, enough to form two teams. The first recorded game of rugby in the town was in 1875. One of the other recently opened businesses in the town, *The Llanelly and County Guardian*, mentions a game at People's Park in 1875 with one team chosen by W. Y. Nevill from the influential shipping family in the town, and the other by Arthur Buchanan, a cashier at the Marshfield works.

Above: LLanelly RFC in the 1880s.
Right: C. W. Mansel Lewis Esq. became President of the club in 1879 and allowed them to mark out part of his Stradey estate as a rugby pitch. The first official game there was against Neath on 29 November 1879.

Some of Morewood's ancestors fought with the House of York in the Wars of the Roses and an ancestor of Rogers' was the first to be martyred by Queen Mary, the original Bloody Mary.

Later that year a meeting was called at The Athenaeum, now the home of Llanelli Library but originally opened with a geological museum and a reading room and intended to be the focus for all sorts of cultural activities in the town, from lectures to musical performances. On 11 November 1875 John Rogers gathered all interested parties together at The Athenaeum to discuss the possibility of forming a rugby club in Llanelli. The idea was accepted wholeheartedly and the first official fixture was arranged just a few weeks later when, on 6 January 1876, Llanelli played the Cambrian Club from Swansea. It was a drawn game. Curiously, the team first played in blue, with high collared jerseys and tight trousers to well under their knee. They also wore Tam O'Shanter-type caps following the use of such headwear in the game between the Nevill and Buchanan XVs, so they could tell one team apart from another. That particular tradition didn't catch on!

'So a rugby club was born! In 1875. Officially.'

So a rugby club was born! In 1875. Officially. But 1972 was hailed as Llanelli's Centenary year. So how did this come about? Well, 1872 is when John D. Rogers came to town with his new game and passion for playing. And there certainly wouldn't be a club if he hadn't. So in one way that is an accurate way of recording the birth of rugby in the town. But as far as the formation of an actual club is concerned, that was done in November 1875. So take your pick.

John Rogers was the team captain for a short period of time before being succeeded by Arthur Buchanan. In that very first season the team played five games, losing one and drawing four. Then, tragically, Buchanan was accidentally killed while out shooting ducks and rugby was suspended. The club went into

Page 22: The Athenaeum, now the home of Llanelli Library. Left: Rhys Gabe. Above: Owen Badger

mourning for six months and not a ball was kicked. The new beginnings faltered.

The response to this tragedy has gone on to be another big part in the story of Llanelli Rugby Club. The game of rugby had obviously captured the imagination of Llanelli's working men, so much so that this break in play proved too much for some. They wanted to keep the momentum going and exercise their new found interest so W. Y. Nevill set about putting a team together in his home village, Felinfoel.

The relationship between village teams in the area and Llanelli Ruby Club has been central right from the start. To this day there remains a strong bond between the likes of Felinfoel, New Dock Stars, Furnace, Bynea, Trimsaran and so many other local village teams and the team that carries the town's name. When, in the 1890s, the club hit its first really difficult patch it was the Seaside Stars, as they were then known, who came to their rescue, supplying Llanelli with much needed players such as

Percy Lloyd and Owen Badger. Also, as with the cricket club, in the early days the practicalities of transport meant the fixture list always featured more local teams, even though the railways were slowly beginning to open up the country.

By 1879, People's Park proved to be inadequate for the growing team's needs. They secured a deal to use the Stradey Cricket Ground, within the estate of Stradey Castle, for both practice and matches. With this arrangement, C. W. Mansel Lewis, the Lord of the Manor at Stradey Castle, became president of the club.

Yet despite the obvious enthusiasm of those who started to pick up this game, not all took to it warmly. For many, it was far too rough a game for a civilised people. Victorian and Nonconformist feathers had been suitably ruffled! The *Western Mail*, twenty years after the club was formed, still referred to displeasure and misgivings about this new craze.

Seven years later, the club had its first international players when Harry Bowen and Alfred Cattell were chosen to play for Wales against England. Ironically, against the backdrop of Tinopolis, both men were teachers. Llanelli provided the Welsh team with players every year after that, with the sole exception of 1900.

Llanelli's reputation as a cup team also started early. The South Wales Challenge Cup started in 1882 and in the first seven years of the competition Llanelli reached the final a remarkable seven times, winning it twice.

The team first wore Scarlet in April 1884, when they played an Irish XV in Llanelli on a Monday following a Wales v Ireland game in Cardiff the Saturday before. A crowd of 5000 spectators saw the Llanelli team play in Scarlet for the first time. Until then the team had worn blue, black, brown and red quarters and primrose and rose — but not all at the same time!

Above: People's Park, where the game was first played in Llanelli.

EASTER HOLIDAYS.

Grand Football Matches !

At the STRADEY GROUNDS, Llanelly.

SATURDAY, April 4th, 1885,
GERMAN GYMNASIUM (LONDON) *v.* LLANELLY.
GOWER ROAD *v.* LLANELLY 2ND XV.

EASTER MONDAY, April 6th, 1885,
DEWSBURY (YORKSHIRE) *v.* LLANELLY.
NEATH 2ND XV. *v.* LLANELLY 2ND XV.

Kick off (each day) at 3.30 p.m.
Admission—SIXPENCE.
No change given at the gate. No dogs allowed on the ground.
Cheap Tickets will be issued by the Great Western Railway to Llanelly, to witness the above Matches, from Swansea, Carmarthen, Llandilo, and all intermediate Stations.
Tickets for the ground may now be obtained of Mr. John Jones, hairdresser, Station Road, Llanelly.

345

GRAND FOOTBALL MATCH!

BATLEY

(The Crack Yorkshire Cup Team)

v.

LLANELLY

On the STRADEY GROUNDS, Llanelly, SATURDAY
NEXT, September 19th, 1885. Kick off at 3.30 p.m.
Admission—SIXPENCE. No Change given at the Gate.
Season Tickets may now be had of the Secretary.

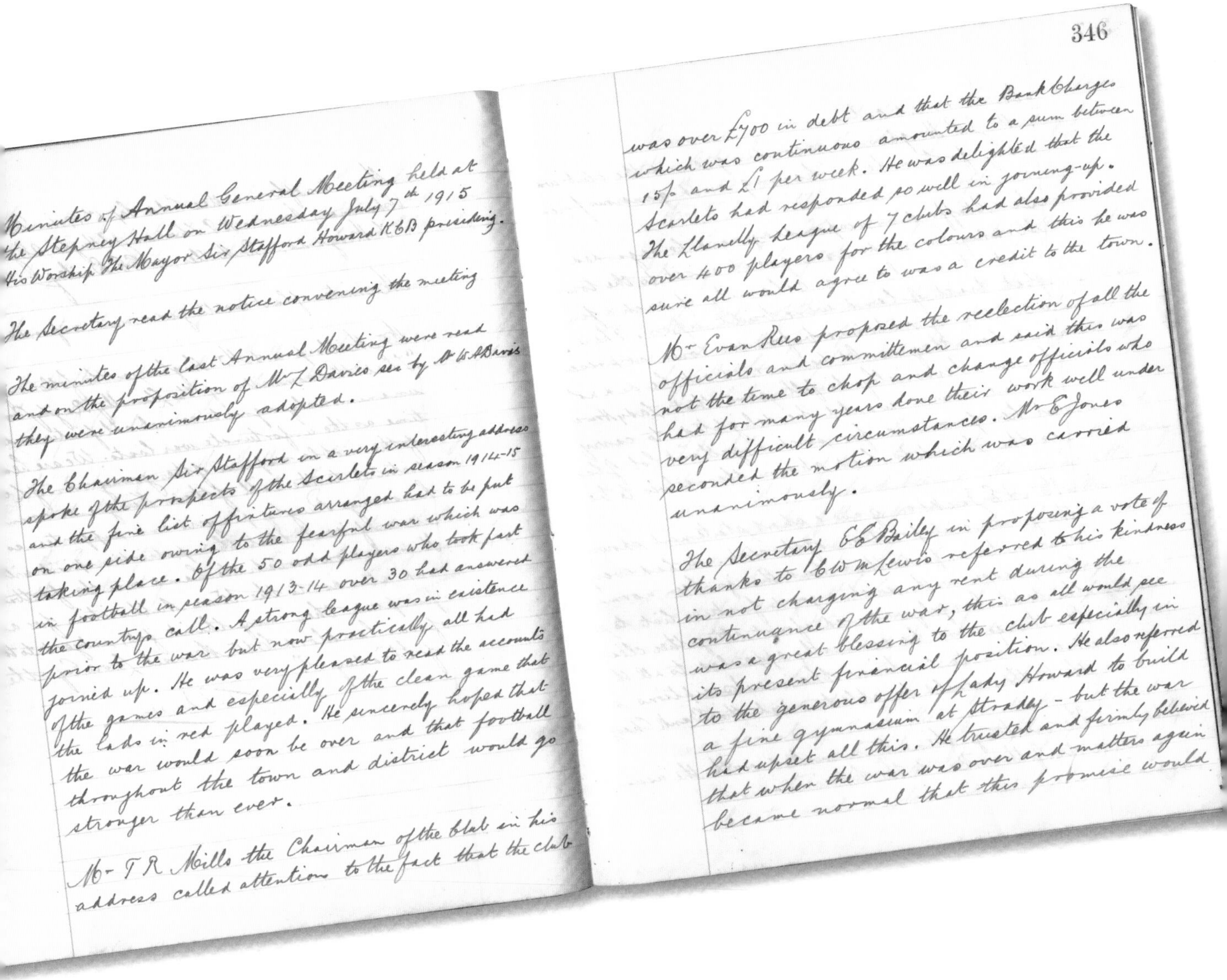

[Handwritten club minutes — left page:]

Minutes of Annual General Meeting held at the Stepney Hall on Wednesday July 7th 1915 His Worship The Mayor Sir Stafford Howard KCB presiding.

The Secretary read the notice convening the meeting

The minutes of the last Annual Meeting were read and on the proposition of Mr L Davies sec by A W Davis they were unanimously adopted.

The Chairman Sir Stafford on a very interesting address spoke of the prospects of the Scarlets in season 1914-15 and the fine list of fixtures arranged had to be put on one side owing to the fearful war which was taking place. Of the 50 odd players who took part in football in season 1913-14 over 30 had answered the country's call. A strong league was in existence prior to the war but now practically all had joined up. He was very pleased to read the accounts of the games and especially of the clean game that the lads in red played. He sincerely hoped that the war would soon be over and that football throughout the town and district would go stronger than ever.

Mr T R Mills the Chairman of the club in his address called attention to the fact that the club

[Handwritten club minutes — right page:]

was over £700 in debt and that the Bank Charges which was continuous amounted to a sum between 15/- and £1 per week. He was delighted that the Scarlets had responded so well in joining-up. The Llanelly League of 7 clubs had also provided over 400 players for the colours and this he was sure all would agree to was a credit to the town.

Mr Evan Rees proposed the reelection of all the officials and committeemen and said this was not the time to chop and change officials who had for many years done their work well under very difficult circumstances. Mr E Jones seconded the motion which was carried unanimously.

The Secretary C C Bailey in proposing a vote of thanks to C W M Lewis referred to his kindness in not charging any rent during the continuance of the war, this as all would see was a great blessing to the club especially in its present financial position. He also referred to the generous offer of Lady Howard to build a fine gymnasium at Stradey – but the war had upset all this. He trusted and firmly believed that when the war was over and matters again became normal that this promise would

The team started to mould rugby heroes from the onset. C. B. Nicholl. Percy Lloyd. Owen Badger – three names still remembered today. The turn of the century brought another wave of stars. Rhys Gabe from Llangennech, who played for Wales in that famous defeat of the All Blacks in 1905; and Harry Watkins, a fireman from Llandovery who also went on to become Chairman of Carmarthenshire County Council and who today has a pub named after him in Felinfoel. And Tom Evans, one of the infamous 'Terrible Eight' who inspired Wales to win three Triple Crowns between 1908 and 1911.

Page 26: 1880 Llanelly team and Newspaper Match advert.
Above: A page from many carefully hand-written volumes of club minutes kept at Llanelli Library.

W. MORRIS   J. JONES   P. J. DAVIES   J. EVANS   D. J. THO

B. JAMES   W. DAVIES   C. BOWEN (Capt)   O. BADGER

D. MORGAN

TEAM.

B. Jenkins   W. J. Thomas
AN Lloyd   M. Williams
B. Davies

Llanelli three-quarter Buckley Roderick once declined an invitation to play for Wales against England so that he could play for Llanelli against Neath on the same day.

Harry Bowen
Hero of the era

Harry Bowen was born in Llanelli in 1864 and, as a boy, lived in a house on the corner of Thomas Street and Prospect Place. He was one of nine children and his dad collected rent. When he had his first cap in 1882 he was a student teacher at Pwll Primary School. His first job as a teacher was in Dewsbury, Yorkshire and while he was there he began a tradition for Llanelli Rugby Club to tour the North of England. The club made many of these tours in the 1880s – quite a venture for the time.

Harry came back to Llanelli and taught in Coleshill School before becoming headmaster of Bynea Primary School.

He captained Llanelli, and later became secretary, treasurer and chairman of the club as well. He was heavily involved in the administration of the game in those early days, being a district representative on the WRU. He picked up the referee's whistle too and took charge of one Calcutta Cup international as well as some of the New Zealand All Blacks games on their very first tour in 1905.

He made one further contribution to rugby as an early rugby journalist, writing for the Cardiff daily, *The Evening Express*. His writing was very literary in style. In a run-up to a Llanelli v Cardiff match, he wrote:

'Everything that has a season has it at Stradey. Cricket and football, pheasants and rabbits, rams and rats, woodpigeons and clay pigeons, and turtledoves persons and birds. There has been more love made in Stradey Woods to the

Choosing a single hero for this era is difficult, as it will be for so many other eras in Llanelli's story. However, because he contributed to so many different aspects in the development of rugby in Llanelli and beyond, the hero on this occasion has to be Harry Bowen.

'With Harry behind the scrum, half our troubles disappear.' So said an editorial in one of the town's newspapers about this most exciting of players. Harry Bowen's place was cemented in the town's story early on, not only because he was one of the first from Llanelli to be capped for Wales but also because he kicked a drop goal to secure victory for Llanelli against the Maoris in 1888 in what was the first ever game played by an overseas touring side in Wales. That's the stuff of rugby legend and Harry deserves his rightful place as one of them.

accompaniment of the cawing of the jackdaws, than in any other place on earth.'

But his match analysis was concise and incisive and it was not unknown for him to write reports of five columns of tightly packed type on just one game.

His last game for Wales was against England at Stradey in 1887. The game was played on the cricket pitch as ice had strangled the rugby field. Harry was the only Llanelli player to play for Wales that day. He died in 1913 aged 49. Harry's hand loomed large on the shaping of the club in those crucial formative years. Nice one, Harry!

The Scarlets played their first game in Europe in 1909 when they went to Paris to play Racing Club de France. They beat them 13-3.

Top: Wales team photo 1890s with C. B. Nicholl.

THE LLANELLY FOOTBALL T

(From a Portrait by J. H. GOLDIE, Swansea).

	W. MORRIS		J. JONES		P. J. DAVIES		J. EVANS		D. J. THOMAS		B
		B. JAMES		W. DAVIES		C. BOWEN (Capt)		O. BADGER		EVAN L
						D. MORGAN				

W. J. Thomas
M. Williams
B. Davies

'In no town in South Wales is so much interest taken in the game as Llanelly; in fact, a match at that town is well worth seeing.' *South Wales Daily News*, February 1884

'It gives me great pleasure to notice not only the good quality and play of the Llanelly team, but also their good morals. I think without exception, I may say that they are all exemplary young men — none of your taproom or pub young fellows… We need not fear the future of Llanelly whilst we have such a fine lot of plucky and good tempered young men, with well-developed frames and exemplary morals. Indeed the county at large also need not fear for its safety, should perchance an enemy invade its shores, whilst we have the determined, indomitable dash of the football players to meet the enemy at the point of the bayonet on their landing.' *Llanelly and County Guardian* 9 December 1880.

Sospan Fach
The song that makes grown men cry!

Welsh

Mae bys Meri-Ann wedi brifo,
A Dafydd y gwas ddim yn iach.
Mae'r baban yn y crud yn crio,
A'r gath wedi sgrabin Joni bach.

Sosban fach yn berwi ar y tân,
Sosban fawr yn berwi ar y llawr,
A'r gath wedi sgrapo Joni bach.
Dai bach y sowldiwr,
Dai bach y sowldiwr,
Dai bach y sowldiwr,
A chwt ei grys e mas.

Mae bys Meri-Ann wedi gwella,
A Dafydd y gwas yn ei fedd;
Mae'r baban yn y crud wedi tyfu,
A'r gath wedi huno mewn hedd.

Sosban fach yn berwi ar y tân
Sosban fawr yn berwi ar y llawr
A'r gath wedi huno mewn hedd.
Dai bach y sowldiwr,
Dai bach y sowldiwr,
Dai bach y sowldiwr,
A chwt ei grys e mas.

Aeth hen Fari Jones i Ffair y Caerau
I brynu set o lestri de;
Ond mynd i'r ffos aeth Mari gyda'i llestri
Trwy yfed gormod lawer iawn o 'de'

Sosban fach yn berwi ar y tân
Sosban fawr yn berwi ar y llawr
A'r gath wedi huno mewn hedd.

English (literal translation)

Mary-Ann has hurt her finger,
And David the servant is not well.
The baby in the cradle is crying,
And the cat has scratched little Johnny.

A little saucepan is boiling on the fire,
A big saucepan is boiling on the floor,
And the cat has scratched little Johnny.
Little Dai the soldier,
Little Dai the soldier,
Little Dai the soldier,
And his shirt tail is hanging out.

Mary-Ann's finger has got better,
And David the servant is in his grave;
The baby in the cradle has grown up,
And the cat is 'asleep in peace'.

A little saucepan is boiling on the fire,
A big saucepan is boiling on the floor,
And the cat is 'asleep in peace'.
Little Dai the soldier,
Little Dai the soldier,
Little Dai the soldier,
And his shirt tail is hanging out.

Old Mary Jones went to the fair in Caerau,
To buy a tea set;
But Mary and her teacups ended up in a ditch,
Through the consumption of rather too much "tea".

A little saucepan is boiling on the fire,
A big saucepan is boiling on the floor,
And the cat is 'asleep in peace'.

The club song's origin has long been claimed by Llanwrtyd Wells, the tiny mid-Wales town. Their Town Council unearthed this early published copy, named 'The Llanwrtyd Anthem' during their centenary celebration in 1995.

In a meeting to commemorate the 50th anniversary of the Llanelli Cymrodorion (a society with the aim of promoting all things Welsh) in October 1942, a talk was given which mentioned that the '…air of 'Sospan Fach' was to be found in the Myvyrian Archaeology — that tome of Welsh poetry and music, and was therefore at least 500 years old.'

Sospan Fach's passion still reverberates round the dressing room walls, keenly felt by players old and new. Here Hanna Morgan leads the singing after a Cup victory against Newport Gwent Dragons in 2013-2014.

'Sospan Fach' does seem to have an extraordinary effect on the Scarlets. The crowd began to sing the Ballad of the Little Saucepan...and instantly the old spirit of the Scarlets began to reassert itself and, before the strains had melted away, they were over with what had seemed an impossible try. It was another testimony to the efficacy of the withered finger and Llanelly's splendid pluck.'
The Cambrian Leader 1896.

From its early days the Llanelli Rugby Club had its own anthem. Having an anthem is important – it's what a team needs to inspire it when things aren't going well or to lead the celebrations when things go according to plan. Llanelli has been inextricably linked with 'Sospan Fach' almost from the very first kick-off.

That's the easy bit. How the song became associated with the club is another story altogether. There are many possible reasons for this, which we'll come to shortly. However, what the song actually means is also a source of confusion. Basically it's about a woman who has hurt her finger, a servant who is not very well and Little Johnny who has been scratched by the cat. Oh, and there's a bit about a soldier with his shirt tails hanging out and a big sospan and a little sospan boiling away nicely on two different fires.

Before we attempt to unravel these mysteries, it's worth pointing out that in no way is this particular kitchen implement ever called a saucepan in Llanelli. It's either sospan in Wenglish or sosban in Welsh.

One thing that is factually evident is that the town was linked to the manufacturing of sospans in that period of frantic industrial activity we heard about earlier. In 1891 The Welsh Tinplate and Metal Stamping Company was opened in the town's North Dock. From here they would send the said implements, dipped in enamel, to the far corners of the world. The factory employed over a thousand Llanelli people; a large proportion of whom were women, an unusual fact in the macho heavy industry world of the time. The factory therefore was a big player in the town and was soon to get bigger as, by the 1920s, it was the biggest of its kind in Britain.

Given this influence it's perhaps no surprise that this simple, practical, every day utensil became the symbol of the town. To the name Tinopolis, Tre'r Sosban (Sospan Town) was soon added. To this day, sospans adorn the top of the rugby posts at Parc y Scarlets as they do the old Stradey posts, now placed in the middle of the Berwick roundabout on the eastern approach to the town and at the Sandy Water Park on the Llanelli Millennium Coast.

Back to the song. To start with, many from the town think that it was written here. The local story claims that it was written in 1889 by Owen Rees of Lakefield Road and that he wrote it in The York Hotel, across the way from People's Park where the team first played. The building no longer exists, but it would have been opposite what is now Wetherspoons, the old York Cinema. Circumstantial evidence, based on the proximity of the pub to where the team played, could back up this claim.

According to this story, Owen Rees wrote it as a response to a request for a song to be performed in a local pantomime. The show, Dick Whittington, was to be in a wooden theatre in Waunlanyrafon, owned by Johnny Noakes. So we do have a Johnny and a cat involved in that story. The problem is that story surfaced in a newspaper in 1934, nearly fifty years later. It still could be true of course, couldn't it?

But one look at other stories relating to the song shows that, far from being local to Llanelli, it was very well travelled indeed. Copies were published in sheet form not long after the club was formed, when it was called the Llanwrtyd Anthem after the spa town in mid-Wales, a popular destination in Victorian times.

The words are based on verse written by Welsh poet Mynyddog in 1873. That was the bardic name of Richard Davies of Llanbrynmair, who published his poem in *Rules of the Hearth* that same year. His verse mentions Catherine Ann being injured, Dafydd y gwas not being very well and that the cat had scraped Joni bach. The refrain urges people to stoke the fire and sing a song in order to keep petty quarrels from the home.

Just over twenty years later, in 1895, an accountant from Dowlais called Talog Williams added his own comic twist to the words while he was working at Llanwrtyd. 'Oh no he didn't!' cried one Reverend D. M. Davies, 'I wrote those words not him!' Thus adding another twist to this tale. Others say that the words were written by a group of drunken students from Bangor University. Or should it be that they read as if they were written by a group of drunken students from Bangor University?

So how did these words and music come from Llanwrtyd? How did the Llanwrtyd Anthem become the anthem of the massed fans of Llanelli Rugby Club? No doubt many Llanelli people would have caught a train to Llanwrtyd in order to enjoy the health spas of that town. It is not too fanciful to imagine them joining in a song that was obviously very well know there. But there's another possible link as well.

One of the club's early stars was flying winger Percy Lloyd who won four caps for Wales between 1890 and 1891. He also kept a hotel in Llanwrtyd. Could he have brought it with him on his travels down to join his fellow Scarlets on match days? It's more than possible.

Percy Lloyd

A very Sixties-influenced instrumental version of Sospan Fach was on the B-side of a single released by chart group The Blackjacks in the early 1960s. There's a jazz version, a folk version and a dance version. Terrace folklore has it that if you slow it right down when you're singing the song, you can fool people to think that you are actually singing a hymn.

The ladies and gents conveniences in award-winning Sosban restaurant at North Dock, Llanelli are labelled Joni Bach and Meri Ann. A very convenient way of keeping the folklore going.

However it came to Llanelli, and when all the heated debate about authorship has settled a little, there can be little disputing that two central parts of this song are, in fact, pure Llanelli, meaning the provenance is, to some extent, guaranteed. Firstly, the obvious references to sospans in title and chorus. That was very much the connection with the Llanelli people.

But what about the reference to Dai bach the soldier with his shirt tails hanging out. This particular soldier was, so the story goes, not called Dai at all but Harold Spiers. During the famous Railway Riots in Llanelli in 1910, he refused to fire at the protesting workers and was thrown out of the army for not obeying orders. Needless to say, the Llanelli people took him to their hearts and gave him a Welsh nickname to boot.

Yet as plausible as it sounds, that might not be true either. The verse referring to Dai bach the

soldier might well have been added at the turn of the century during the time of the Boer War. When the song, in some versions, refers to his shirt tails sticking out, a question is asked as to what kind of shirt it was. The reply is that it was a white shirt with a blue stripe, referring to the traditional working man's flannel shirt of the time. This answer is greeted by a request that the shirt be tucked back in, to which the reply is 'no, I'd rather leave it out!' The club recently produced a blue and white stripe shirt as part of its official merchandise. Now you know why.

Yet another twist suggests that Dai wasn't even a soldier, the original line actually refers to him as Dai bach y soldrwr, the solderer who would have been responsible for soldering the handles on to the sospans in the aforementioned Stamping Works. So you choose your words and you sing your song!

There is actually a third, and maybe even a fourth, direct Llanelli link. After the team beat the touring Australians in 1908, the 'Who Beat the Wallabies?' verse was added. That verse now covers all four occasions Llanelli have beaten the team from Down Under. Then, in 1972, 'Who Beat the All Blacks?' was another welcome addition to the 'Sospan Fach' canon.

After the 1908 game there's a reference to the song in an Australian newspaper. One of the 1908 Australian team, forward Tom Richards, mentioned in the *Sydney Mail* in his report of the game against Llanelli that 'Sospan Fach' was sung by the fans during the match. It obviously made quite an impression in him.

For all the discussions and arguments as to the exact origin, this report in an Australian newspaper surely gives a clear indication that the song was already well and truly established as the club's song within thirty years of it being formed. Whatever the origin, the meaning, or even the words you choose to sing, the song remains the same!

The Team that Defeated the Wallabies.

LLANELLY v. AUSTRALIANS, October 17th, 1908.

LLANELLY 1 Goal 1 Try, AUSTRALIANS 1 Try.

BACK ROW. T. R. MILLS. J. WATTS. J. AUCKLAND. D. L. BOWEN. A. J. STACEY. W. COLE. IKE LEWIS. W. J. THOMAS.

T. MILLAR.

SITTING. H. RICHARDS. REV. T. WILLIAMS. T. EVANS (CAPT). H. THOMAS. W. THOMAS.

IN FRONT. D. LLOYD. H. MORGAN. W. ARNOLD. W. H. DAVIES.

After the team beat the touring Australians
in 1908, the 'Who Beat the Wallabies?'
verse was added.

The Era of Giants
1918–1939

The First World War stopped play in Llanelli as it did throughout the rugby and sport-playing world. At least, that is, as far as official fixtures were concerned. Many matches were still played unofficially.

When fixtures resumed, the Llanelli centre was Bryn Williams. He recalls the men of the town arriving back from the Front on the outbreak of peace, and facing a dilemma.

'When the First World War was over, many of the ex-servicemen in the town met in the Barley Mow public house in Market Street to decide whether it was rugby or soccer they would play regularly. A number of us chose rugby and for a season we played under the name 'Demobbed

Soldiers'. We were unbeaten, and our record included a drawn match against Llanelli!'

Bryn Williams then played for Llanelli for one season, partnering Albert Jenkins at centre, before going north to play Rugby League.

Once fixtures resumed a true golden era opened up for Llanelli RFC. What a twenty years it proved to be before World War guns would be heard once again. The 1920s specifically have earned the title The Era of Giants in the club's history. And these were giants in a land of very big people.

If you think sharing the club captaincy between two players is a modern innovation then you need to think again. The first season after

W. H. Clement

Ivor Jones

hostilities ended Llanelli had two captains, Dick Edmunds and Dai Hiddlestone.

The former was the main person instrumental in keeping the game ticking over during the war years. A story in the *Western Mail* in September 1920, credits his contribution.

'Immediately prior to the War, rugby at Llanelli was somewhat stale, but thanks to Mr Dick Edmunds, the interest was not allowed to die. During the whole period of hostilities, Mr Edmunds, notwithstanding great difficulties, kept the game going with the result that after signing the Armistice, the Llanelly Club was able to arrange fixtures with several Colonial sides as well as the RAF and the RND, and the United Services.'

The report goes on to say that these increased fixtures helped to revive rugby at Llanelli, and clear the club's debts as well. As a result, the club avoided the possibility of losing their support, and interest in the club and the game generally, after such a long period of having to suspend all its usual activities.

The club was in very good hands after that as a glance at the list of captains reveals. For twelve seasons, up until 1939-40, the leaders on the pitch were a certain Jenkins, Jones and Clement. Not a company of solicitors in

Star player Ivor Jones played 522 games for the Scarlets, finishing playing just before the start of the Second World War. In total, he scored 1,349 points for the club. Only three players have ever played 500 games for the club. Ivor Jones, Laurance Delaney (500) and Phil May (551).

town, but none other than Albert Jenkins, Ivor Jones and W. H. Clement. Ivor Jones captained his club for eight seasons, a record that still stands today. Many players since then have captained the club for four, five or six seasons, which shows that loyalty and continuity have been highly valued at the club. Add Elvet Jones and F. L. Morgan to that inter-war captains list and it becomes evident that the club had solid leadership on the field of play for a very long period.

The club also supplied Wales with 36 internationals during this period, a period when they would only play against seven other countries in the world; once a year in the case of the home nations, less against the Southern Hemisphere countries. Ivor Jones played in

16 internationals between 1924 and 1930 and Albert Jenkins in 14 between 1920 and 1928.

Ivor Jones left a lasting legacy on the game he loved and played so well. His first match for the club was in 1922 in the traditional Boxing Day fixture against London Welsh. He went on to score over 1,200 points in his career, 237 of those in one season! A wing-forward, he can be credited with developing the style of play we are used to in that position today. His approach was modern for his time with emphasis on ball carrying and more open wing-forward play. He dominated the long throws in lines-out, was great at controlling the ball with his feet, was quick to the breakdown and a ferocious tackler. Indeed, he wouldn't be out of place in today's back row game.

He also has another claim to fame, being the first Llanelli player to be chosen for what is now known as The British and Irish Lions. In the 1929-1930 season, he toured with the British Isles team to New Zealand and Australia. He played in all five Testmatches and created quite an impression, soon being given a nickname by the New Zealanders, 'The King'. No, Barry John wasn't the first!

Opposition to the formation of a rugby club in the town was still to be heard in this era as well. Archie Skym wasn't allowed to play rugby until he was eighteen because of his father's religious views. In this case the paternal restraint ultimately proved ineffective as this back row forward not only turned out for Llanelli but went on to play twenty times for his country and earn the nickname, 'The Butcher'!

This era of success and big rugby stars kept the club safe in the face of another very real threat as well. Rugby League was growing in its appeal and its influence was spreading. Commenting on the club's fortunes at the beginning of a new decade a *Western Mail* article says that the club has:

...risen at times to giddy heights, and at other periods it has fallen into an abyss. It knows the inexpressible joy of having an all but invincible season, and it also knows the despondency created by ignominious defeats, but throughout, the public of Llanelly have remained steadfast to the Welsh national pastime, and even now when the sister code is making such inroads in most parts of South Wales the position of rugby in 'Sospanville' is stronger than ever.

Above: Llanelli 1920-21 team photo.
Right (top): Llanelly v Neath Programme 28th November 1936. Right (bottom): Llanelly v Bath Programme 8th October 1938.

LLANELLY.			NEATH.	
(1) R. G. BROWN	Full Back	C. JONES	(1)
(2) W. H. CLEMENT	Left Wing	M. CLEMENT	(5)
(3) G. ELIAS	Left Centre	S. HARRIS	(4)
(4) F. REES	Right Centre	E. WALTERS	(3)
(5) E. L. JONES (Capt.)	Right Wing	H. POWELL	(2)
(6) W. R. J. JONES	Outside Half	F. REES	(7)
(7) A. R. SMITH	Inside Half	D. PARKER	(6)
(8) W. H. WILLIAMS	Forwards	H. THOMAS (Capt.)	(8)
*(9) B. EVANS	,,	T. MORGAN	(9)
(10) E. EVANS	,,	E. MORGAN	(10)
(11) J. L. C. MORGAN	,,	W. DAVIES	(11)
(12) Dr. E. N. REES	,,	L. JAMES	(12)
(13) B. J. BOWEN	,,	D. L. THOMAS	(14)
(14) S. WILLIAMS	,,	A. McCARLEY	(15)
*(15) IFOR E. JONES	,,	C. CHALLINOR	(16)

Colours: Scarlet. * Denotes Internationals.

Colours—Black with White Maltese Cross.

Linesman—Dr. H. D. LLEWELLYN.

Linesman—Mr. R. DAVIES.

REFEREE ... Mr. J. W. FAULL, Morriston.

Next Home Match: 19th Dec., v. PONTYPOOL. Kick-off, 2.45

STRADEY PARK, LLANELLY.
Price One Penny. —:0:— No. 1166

Official Programme

BATH v. LLANELLY
Saturday, October 8th, 1938.
Kick-off at 3.15 p.m.

45

Albert Jenkins
Hero of the era

An era of giants throws up many candidates, many of whom have been mentioned already. But one does stand out, a man who has reached legendary status in the club's history. Albert Jenkins. He was a star, very much an individual who expressed himself on the field of play and mixed very little with his team-mates off the pitch. The word enigmatic comes to mind, as with many real stars.

He was born in Llanelli in 1895 and was enthused by the game that was rapidly taking root in his home town. He played junior rugby but the war interrupted his playing and he was soon off to France to fight with the 38th Welsh Division. He played rugby for them whenever possible. In 1919 he played for Llanelli who moved this, until then full-back, to centre. A shrewd move.

Like so many of his fellow players before and after he worked in the tinplate industry. In this sense he was right at the heart of the traditional link between the club and the town's heavy industry. This, no doubt, contributed to his greatest asset as a player, his physique. He had strong, powerful shoulders, chest and thighs. Add to this, speed and an ability to swerve that big physique with remarkable agility and it was a fine athlete who took to the fields of Stradey each matchday. No surprise that he caught the eye and proved popular with the Scarlet faithful. He was one of the very early players who, as the rather more modern phrase would have it, put bums on seats.

Four months after starting to play for Llanelli, the Welsh selectors came calling. He represented his country for the first time in 1920 against England. He scored for Wales in the next game against Scotland and shone in the following game against Ireland, scoring another try and creating three for his Llanelli team-mate, Bryn Williams. Albert Jenkins had most definitely arrived.

He was also master of the drop goal, as he showed many times for both club and country. He captained Wales for the first time against Ireland in 1923 but that wasn't such a good year for the Welsh team. For the first time since 1892 they lost to all the home nations in a single season. Not a bad record, thirty years without losing to all the home countries, but still one that is not pleasant to lose.

The following year he shone as his club took on the mighty All Blacks. Llanelli only lost 8-3 and it was one of those games that will go down in rugby folklore as having been lost as a result of lots of obstruction and offside on the part of the All Blacks! It was a different story when the next opposition from New Zealand visited Stradey. The Maoris arrived in 1926 and Llanelli beat them 3-0. They then went on to beat the Waratahs in 1927 with Jenkins unstoppable through all these games.

In the 1927-1928 season, Llanelli became the Welsh club champions for the first time in thirty years. The club supplied six players for the international against Scotland that year with Jenkins again inspirational in that game. He scored a try and drove his country on to victory. By then he was 33 years old and hadn't played for Wales for the previous four years.

They refer to Albert Jenkins as both a prince and a god in Llanelli rugby country and who would argue against either? Unfortunately for this divine prince he was around at a time when things weren't too good for Welsh international rugby. Eventually he was offered £375 pounds to leave the Scarlets and head north to join Wigan Rugby League. However, he turned the move down, electing instead to stay loyal to his home town club whatever the money offered by others.

He died when he was 58 years old and was given the honour of a civic funeral, with the mayor and his chains officially present. Thousands of Llanelli people filled the streets that day to say goodbye to a true Scarlet hero.

Seaside Stars team 1928 with Albert Jenkins. Below: Albert Jenkins tribute 1950.

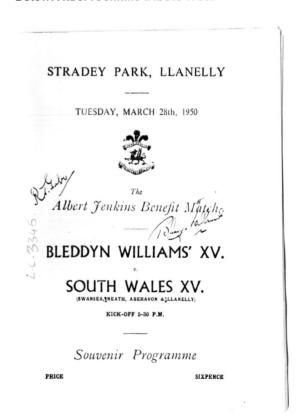

STRADEY PARK, LLANELLY

TUESDAY, MARCH 28th, 1950

The
Albert Jenkins Benefit Match

BLEDDYN WILLIAMS' XV.

v.

SOUTH WALES XV.
(SWANSEA, NEATH, ABERAVON & LLANELLY)

KICK-OFF 5-30 P.M.

Souvenir Programme

PRICE   SIXPENCE

The tough economical hardships of the Twenties hit the club as well. The club were in dire financial straits and decided that one money saving measure to be taken was not to put numbers on the back of the shirts.

The Supporters Club was formed in 1920. Membership was two shillings (ten pence) and you could get a badge as well if you paid an extra one shilling and sixpence (seven and a half pence today).

In 1920 fruit and programmes were also sold for the first time on match day. That's also when the tradition of playing Bath for the rag doll started.

Left: Llanelli in 1929.
Above: Grav ready to grab the rag doll back from Bath's hands!

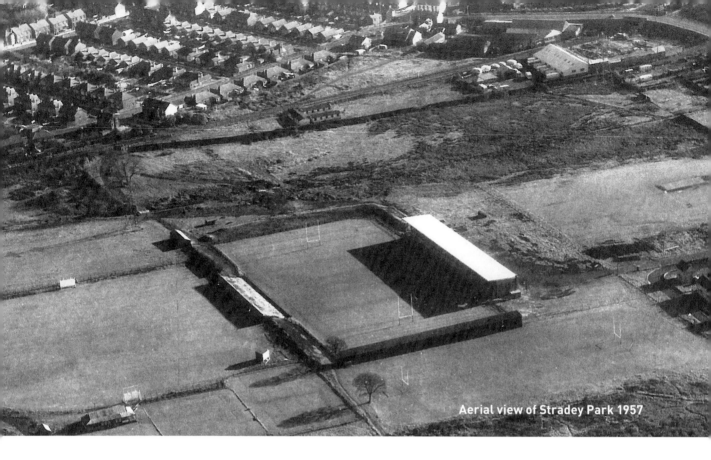

Aerial view of Stradey Park 1957

Stradey Park
The place, the power and the passion

It's a Mecca, a cathedral, a site of pilgrimage known throughout the world as one of the leading rugby grounds. Stradey. The site of many a famous victory, crushed touring teams, broken hearts, shattered expectations, silky side-steps, banter worthy of literary merit, grunts and thuds of pounding forwards that shook the Celtic earth, fast, open, cultured handling and of course, blinding performances by referees. It holds a strong emotional place in the heart of the community it served for such a long period of time.

The name goes back to Roman times. Stradey comes from the same word as Strata in Strata

Florida Abbey in Mid Wales, meaning 'road' or 'way', and this particular Roman road would have passed roughly where the Stradey Arms pub is today, through the current Stradey Estate and west to Moridunum, or Carmarthen as we know it. Some years later, when the Romans were long gone, an estate was built on land near this road and the Stradey Estate developed as a central feature of Llanelli and Carmarthenshire social and political life.

But back to rugby. At the end of the nineteenth century the growing Llanelli rugby club needed somewhere to play their matches. People's Park was proving impractical as it was used for other activities as well as rugby and the rugby club didn't have full control over the space.

In 1877, the South Wales Challenge Cup was introduced and the first Llanelli games in this competition were at People's Park. But this was not going to be a ground suitable for any sustained cup success. Also, in 1878, local by-laws were being tightened to regulate the use of the park. They didn't refer directly to rugby at that time, but things were changing and an answer was needed that best suited the club. That answer came in 1879 when the Squire of Stradey, Mr. C. W. Mansel Lewis, agreed to let the club use some of the ground within his estate. This was near, and sometimes on, an existing cricket pitch near the Cille brook, alongside the original Furnace Primary School. Mr. Mansel Lewis then became President of the club.

So, in another strange quirk of fate, this public school game which the industrial workers of Llanelli made their very own, now turned back to the gentry for some land on which to play.

Llanelli won the South Wales Challenge Cup in 1884. Subsequently, the first grandstand was built at the ground in 1886 for the princely sum of £150. This move also brought international rugby to the town for the first time as there was now a pitch that could showcase the very best. That was in January 1887 and Wales were to play England with Llanelli hero Harry Bowen, the Welsh full-back. Other internationals were to follow and to this day it's the only ground where Wales have never been beaten!

The choice of Stradey as the venue for that 1887 international, and the broader Welsh reaction to it, says a lot about the growing influence of the town in Welsh rugby. The authorities evidently thought that Llanelli deserved to be chosen, that it was a significant enough location on the Welsh rugby map to be given an international. On the other hand, other Welsh clubs weren't so sure and questioned the choice of Llanelli,

Old Stradey Park entrance gates.

In 1891, Wales won the Triple Crown for the first time, beating Ireland 3–0. 20,000 were at Stradey to witness this milestone.

In 1927 there was a proposal to introduce greyhound racing to Stradey. It didn't happen.

saying it had been given an 'honour beyond its deserts'. There was significant lobbying to the WRU for the decision to be reversed. In the club's defence, and indeed the town's, the local press rallied:

We must perforce concede that Llanelly cannot afford equal facilities with Cardiff or Newport, but it is to be remembered that we possessed unique claims to the coveted honour. Where has football found a more congenial soil than at Llanelly? Where in South Wales is the town in which the winter pastime has become so interwoven with the social life of the inhabitants?

This question is then followed by a wonderful piece of partisan rhetoric:

We will not pause for a reply, because reply there is none.

Stradey
Park

Aerial view of Llanelli after World War Two.

This interchange is an early example of the east-west internal rivalry that has been present in Welsh rugby matters ever since. It's also an early example of the need for Llanelli to develop an attacking form of defence, which has sometimes been interpreted as arrogance of the one-eyed kind.

If there were any lingering doubts about Llanelli and Stradey's suitability for international matches they were dealt a further blow in 1888 when Llanelli beat the first ever touring team to

Britain, the Maoris. Scarlet Fever was, by then, official.

Llanelli played on this land until 1904. On 15 October that year, the land that developed to be the world renowned Stradey was officially opened. The original Stradey pitch had 'got into a very rough state' as one local paper put it. The announcement of this move also referred to great plans, on behalf of the Llanelli Rugby Club Committee, to develop the facilities there and to build a grandstand. This was a club that was going places.

The team would have to use the facilities of many local hostelries for changing before matches, as well as for functions and team socialising. They used the Barley Mow pub in Market Street, (alongside the current Altalia restaurant), the Prince of Wales in Hall Street, and the Stradey Arms in Furnace. They would be taken from these places to the match on a horse-brake (a horse-drawn carriage). Another pub used was the Stag's Head, from which there was a footpath to Stradey through Caer Elms.

Official functions were often at The Salutation Hotel, next to the library as it was then, where the 1970s extension now stands. This was used as the club headquarters for many years along with The Thomas Arms. There is also mention of some players using the room of a local hotel as a place to do their exercises during the week and before matches.

From these humble and difficult beginnings, what followed in this rugby cauldron over the following decades turned into rugby folklore renowned the world over. And there were to be three further major steps in the Stradey story – the story of the stadium itself, that is, rather than the action on the pitch.

As the end of the 1940s approached, Stradey had two large iron gates and five small doors at its entrance; a wooden grandstand backing on to Sandy Road which was accessed through a large door at the town end, and the more recent addition – built ready for the game against the Springboks in 1931 – of a steel and corrugated iron stand at the Pwll End, an extension of the wooden one. This extension housed committee rooms, baths and changing rooms. The site was still relatively small however, and the branches of many surrounding pine trees were used to watch games, with the expected result of many a fall from these trees during more exciting passages of play!

However, by the 1950s there was a need to further develop facilities at the ground. In 1952

The Thomas Arms was the club's unofficial HQ for years.

a development programme was launched and six and a half acres of Stradey Park was bought for £6,500. This included the pitch and the grandstand. In 1953 a terraced bank was built for £5,000. In 1957, a brand new grandstand was opened at a cost of £14,500. And in 1959, a new clubhouse was opened, which cost £5,000. That's more than £30,000 worth of investment, a significant sum of money for the time and a clear sign of the Llanelli Committee's pioneering vision.

The next big step in the Stradey story is not such a happy one. We're now in the 1990s and the game throughout the UK has turned professional. There's big money around, millionaire backers on the scene, players officially being paid and sponsorship encouraged on a grand scale. But clubs throughout the land found the transition difficult and Llanelli was no exception.

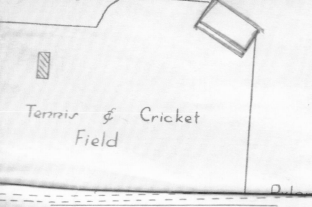

Tennis & Cricket
Field

Cille
Cottage

Rugby Football
Field

Stradey Park groundsman, Dan Long, used to ask fans to pay two pence before he would return any walking stick dropped from the grandstand.

Rabaiotti and Sons were allowed into Stradey to sell fish and chips in 1911.

The Royal Welsh Show was at Stradey in 1931 and the Prince of Wales paid a visit.

In 1935 Stradey's future was in jeopardy – there were plans to build houses on the site.

The first four point try scored at Stradey was by hooker Roy Thomas in 1971. He was unlucky enough to be on the subs bench 24 times for Wales without ever getting capped.

Plans to modernise Stradey, drawn up in 1950 and the handing over of the key when the job was done. The architect, W. J. Walters on the right, hands the key to W. John Thomas, the club's vice-president.

To Llanelly

A. B. Richards A.M.I.C
Borough Engineer
Llanelly
27.III.50

South Wales Evening Post

Stradey improvements will cost £10,000

Early start likely

CLUB HOPES THAT FUND WILL PICK UP

UNLESS the Stradey appeal fund begins to pick up, the Llanelly Rugby Club will be very much "in the red" by this time next year. The present aim is to complete ground improvements which are liable to cost the best part of £10,000, in time for the visit of the New Zealand touring team in November, 1953.

There has been a recent change in the development set-up, and the man now virtually in charge of the improvements programme is Mr. Handel Rogers.

This is a wise move as Mr. Rogers is the only member of the club committee who is by occupation a businessman. He is energetic and enterprising, and there is no doubt in my mind that things will really begin to move at Stradey if he is given

By Scarlet

a free hand and a reasonable measure of practical support by his colleagues.

I am informed that recent discussions which have taken place with the club trustees and other interested parties have resulted in the development plan being amended in certain details and that a start on the work is to be made immediately.

New entrance

One of the first jobs will be to make a new main entrance to the ground. This will be about 30-40 yards from the present gates and will face the approach road along Stradey Park-avenue. There will be two large gates and eight smaller entrances from which a road will run down to a new bridge to be built over the stream that runs parallel to the boundary

An *Evening Post* story in October 1952 by that prolific journalist and ex-Scarlets scrum-half, Harry 'Scarlet' Davies.

The Tanner Bank boys – and girls!

THE SCARLETS

30p

-V-

ABERAVON

Saturday, 22nd February, 1986. Kick-Off 3.00 p.m.

Above: A bird's eye view of the Stradey legacy. A full to capacity stadium and behind the rugby, the cricket pitch and tennis club – a testimony to sport for generations of Llanelli people, thanks to the Stradey estate.

Right: A gathering of some former presidents, chairmen, coaches, captains and players as the club says farewell to Stradey. After the game, the champagne flows to mark the end of an era.

The last ever game at Stradey was on 24 October 2008. It was an EDF Energy Cup game and Scarlets beat Bristol 27–0 on an emotional occasion, filled with fireworks, an array of former captains and an assembly of choirs.

Top: The grand old lady the night before the last game, no doubt looking back over her shoulder at the heritage she was part of. Above: The foundation of the scoreboard that recorded many famous victories was the last trace of Scarlet before houses were built on the site.

The club's venture into the big name signings that were now permissible was to go for Frano Botica, the former All Black, who played rugby league for Wigan, and who was, by 1996, playing for Orrell. He was brought to Llanelli for a huge sum, one that many Premier League footballers would be happy with. But it was a step too far. The sums couldn't add up and Llanelli was facing the very real threat of extinction due to failure to pay debts. There was only one answer, they had to sell Stradey to the Welsh Rugby Union for £1.25 million. A scheme was devised to offer shares to Scarlets fans in order to raise money to stop the club from going under. Under professional guidance, this scheme worked and, by 2005, Stradey was back in the club's hands. The fervour and passion of the fans had saved the club.

The third step was the final one, literally, when it was decided that Stradey was no longer suitable to cope with professional, regional rugby. A new ground had to be found and this was to prove really difficult for so many of the Scarlets faithful. To think of leaving such a place was not going to be easy. Years of history, heritage and emotional attachment was significant baggage that would not be shed readily. But the decision was made in the knowledge that there was no way the club could advance if it remained at a ground that wasn't fit for purpose anymore. Parc y Scarlets was declared to be the name of the new stadium on 20 May 2008 and it was officially opened in November that year. The official opening match was on 31 January 2009 when Llanelli defeated the Barbarians 40-24. It cost £23 million to construct, and was designed by the same company who designed Murrayfield in Edinburgh. Ironically, they had to go out of town to get the structural steel needed to build it. It seems the town has undergone a few changes too.

After nearly 130 years, the link between rugby and Stradey had come to an end.

No doubt the most remarkable event held at Stradey was the funeral of the great Ray Gravell. 15 November 2007. Up to 10,000 people from far and wide were present, among them the First Minister of Wales, the Archdruid of Wales, public figures from literature and broadcasting, and many rugby legends from many countries. His flag-draped coffin was carried by six international players across a red carpet on the pitch and the scoreboard showed Llanelli 9 Seland Newydd 3 as it did on the day when Grav was the youngest member of the team that beat the All Blacks in 1972. He died 35 years to the very day of that victory. Tributes, songs and silence reverberated around the ground in a state-like homage to a larger than life man; an event that was unprecedented in rugby stadiums.

The Magnificent Seven and a Fistful of Stars

1945-1959

The Second World War ended, men returned to the town and the process of rebuilding normal life began. Two early milestones in the town's story after the war were the opening in 1947 of Ysgol Dewi Sant, the first state Welsh medium Primary School in Wales, and the announcement by The Steel Company of Wales soon after that Trostre Cold Mill was to be built as a part of a massive national expansion. Not long after Trostre opened in 1954 German technicians moved in to begin work on developing the Cynheidre Colliery site on the outskirts of town.

In 1950, the first television programme was received in the town – a circus act televised from the Sutton Coldfield TV station. Two amateur radio buffs started to devise a television set, independently of each other, but they came together just before the end and pooled resources and ideas to form the first TV in town. No doubt they had lots of friends from then on!

On the pitch, a new era was about to begin. If there were giants in the previous era, there were many in this one as well. The Scarlets enhanced their reputation as a leading force in world club rugby a process which started almost as soon as the last echoes of the war had died away. The 1946-1947 season saw Llanelli provide the Welsh team with seven players who were, not surprisingly, called The Magnificent Seven in those cowboy loving days. They were Griff Bevan, who was the team's first captain after the war; Howard Davies, the full-back, who had also been capped before the war; Handel Greville and Peter Rees – both of whom went on to be chairmen of Llanelli rugby club; Stan Williams, who went on to be a long serving committee member; the wing-forward Ossie Williams and the centre or wing, Les Williams. The last two have been called among the best to have played for the club since World War Two. Not a bad accolade if you consider all the other candidates. The Home Nations of 1947 was the first since 1931 to include France as well – they had been kicked out following allegations of professionalism. The Five Nations stayed unbroken from 1947 to 2000, when Italy made it six.

On the hallowed Stradey turf, the forwards dominated the role of captain for most of the late Forties and Fifties. The backs didn't get much of a look in. Twelve Scarlets led their team between 1946 and 1960 and eight of them were forwards. They were Griff Bevan, Peter Evans, Des Jones, Ken Jones, Ossie Williams, Allan Jones, R. H. Williams and Howard 'Ash' Davies. These were the men who, literally, led from the front, putting their club at the top of

The 1946–1947 season saw Llanelli provide the Welsh team with seven players, who were not surprisingly called, in those cowboy loving days, The Magnificent Seven.

Top row: Handel Greville, Peter Rees, Stan Williams.
Middle: Les Williams, Howard Davies, Griff Bevan.
Left: Ossie Williams. The Magnificent Seven.

club rugby. All but two, Ken Jones and Alan Jones, played for Wales. Howard 'Ash' Davies was capped in 1947 against England, having not played for Wales since the game against Ireland in 1939.

The backs who broke this forward dominance of Llanelli club captains were Handel Greville, Ray Williams, Wynne Evans and Onllwyn Brace. These men were stars who embodied the free spirit associated with the club. Each one played for Wales. Not a bad record indeed – ten of the twelve club captains in a fourteen-year period were chosen to play for their country.

Llanelli players didn't only make their mark on club and country either. On the broader, worldwide rugby field two Llanelli players created British and Irish Lions records in this era. Lewis Jones became the youngest ever British Lion when he was chosen to tour New Zealand in 1950. He was just eighteen years old!

R. H. Williams became the first forward to play ten consecutive tests for the British and Irish Lions. He played four against South Africa in 1955, four against New Zealand and two against Australia on the 1959 tour. Two remarkable achievements.

If the Forties gave us the Magnificent Seven, the Fifties nearly did as well, but fell just one short. The 1958 team gave Wales six players for the team to face the touring Australians that year. They were Wynne Evans, Carwyn James, Ray Williams, Terry Davies, Cyril Davies and R. H. Williams. This game saw the debuts of half-back pair Wynne Evans and Carwyn James. The outside-half, who would famously go on to coach the club, dropped a goal in a 9-3 victory for Wales.

Above top row: Arthur John, Ernie Finch, Albert Jenkins, Dai John. Bottom row: Iorwerth Jones, Ivor Jones, Archie Skym. The 1920s' Magnificent Seven.

Right, top row: Ray Williams, Cyril Davies, Wynne Evans. Seated: Carwyn James, Handel Rogers (Chairman) R. H. Williams. In front: Terry Davies. The Magnificent Llanelli six who played for Wales against Australia in 1958.

We haven't even mentioned two megastars of this era yet! Terry Davies and Lewis Jones; two players who not only set Stradey alight, but world rugby also and, in Jones' case, the other rugby code up north as well.

They say that a move by one player can change the fortunes of his team, be it club or country. Lewis Jones proved that to be true. The young eighteen-year-old full-back had been picked to play for Wales against the old enemy, England, on 21 January 1950. He gathered the ball from an English attacking kick but, instead of putting in an up-field clearance kick, he decided to run with the ball – a bit like Benny for the Baa-Baas against the All Blacks before 'that try'. He ran diagonally into open space to his left, straightened, swerved through his supposed tacklers and ran back to the right. The ball went out to Malcolm Thomas and Cliff Davies before Bob Evans crossed for a try. Magic! It put Wales on the road for a victory in that game, only their second in Twickenham in 40 years and on then to their first Triple Crown in 39 years. Lewis

Left: What it's all about! A group of eager fans admire Terry Davies' kicking action. Above: Lewis Jones, one of the best players of the modern era.

Jones, rather unsurprisingly, was carried off the pitch at HQ that day.

Later that year he flew out as a replacement to join the Lions tour of New Zealand and Australia. He scored 63 points in seven games on that tour – one try, two penalties, two conversions and a 50 yard dropped goal. He went on to be a firm favourite at Stradey, creating as many tries as he scored himself. He was worshipped by the fans in the same way as Albert Jenkins had been. But he didn't

shine at Llanelli for long. In 1952 he went north, joining Leeds and staying with them for twelve seasons. In the 1956-1957 season, he smashed the Rugby League points scoring record for one season, scoring a massive 505 points!

And then there's Terry Davies. A genius before his time, who the All Blacks of the late Fifties said was worthy of taking his place in any international team in the world. That's some accolade. This Bynea boy started playing for Swansea, then did his National Service in the Navy, from where he earned his first international caps, and then back to Swansea. A serious shoulder injury kept him out of the game for over two years before he joined Llanelli in 1956 where he stayed until 1961. He played in two Test matches for the British and Irish Lions on their New Zealand tour of 1959. He finished the whole tour with 104 points from 13 matches.

R. H. Williams
Hero of the era

So many have already been mentioned, but one probably stands out more than the others. All Black legend Colin Meads said of this man that if he was born in New Zealand, he would have been an All Black. Others have referred to him as probably the best second row to wear a Welsh jersey and definitely the best second row to pull on a Lions jersey, even greater than the legendary five times Lion, Willie John McBride. It is, of course, R.H. Williams. Such praise goes a long way to justify his inclusion as the hero of this era.

Born in Cwmllynfell, he went to Ystalyfera Grammar School, the same school as Claude Davey who captained Wales in their victory over the All Blacks in 1935. He was called a giant of a player, standing at 6 foot two and a half and weighing 16 stone. How the game has changed – that's a scrum-half these days!

He first played for Llanelli in 1949 when he was 19 years old. He graduated from Cardiff University, which is where he said his love for the Scarlets was kindled following a game between Cardiff University and Pontyberem. As a result of that game he struck up a friendship with Scarlet Ossie Williams and the rest, as they say, is history.

He then went to be an education officer in the RAF, but still played for Llanelli occasionally while he was with the forces. But he didn't make his mark with the club until he started playing regularly in the mid-1950s.

Speaking over twenty years after retiring from the game, he said, *'I can still recall the excitement of arriving at Stradey on Saturday afternoons and experiencing the tingling feeling prior to playing against Swansea Neath or Aberavon. All other games apart, four games with each of these clubs – the vogue in those days – convinced one that only the strong of heart and constitution could survive.'* He went on to say that the greatest joy of his year as captain, 1957-1958, was beating Swansea on all four occasions!

He had his first Welsh cap in 1954 against Ireland. R. H. was one of those stars who was destined to play for his country at a time when it wasn't doing too well. He played regularly from 1956 until 1960, but it wasn't the best period for Wales as England and France were dominating. However, he won 23 caps and earned his place amongst the rugby greats.

He certainly gave thousands of fans a definite tingling feeling that broke out into Scarlet Fever over the many years he played for both his club and his country.

Wales were heading to win the Triple Crown against England in 1958. A last minute Terry Davies kick would have secured the victory. But it hit the post. Some aggrieved Welsh fans' response is now very much part of rugby folklore as they kidnapped the offending crossbar and brought it back to Wales. On their way, they bumped in to Terry and his wife in a café in the Cotswolds. They promptly fetched the woodwork from their vehicle and asked him to sign it. The bemused and amused Terry obliged, but he also contacted HQ and offered to make them a new one — he had a timber merchant's business in Bynea. His offer was politely refused, with some undertones of 'you don't really think we want a Welsh crossbar in Twickers do you.' The crossbar kidnappers allegedly came from west of Llanelli, but we couldn't possibly verify if they were Scarlets fans or not, though there is rumour that the piece of crossbar is in a pub in Cresswell, Pembrokeshire.

In 1942, the first British Restaurant opened in Llanelli, the fiftieth in Wales. Decorated in British Restaurant colours of cream and blue, it took over half the space in the lesser Market Hall.

Between 1947 and 1959, 25 Scarlets played for Wales, winning over 140 caps.

In 1947 the club had a then record 1783 members. For some unfathomable reason the figure dropped to 700 next season but it soon picked up again.

The Machynys Foundry opened in the spring of 1952. It covered twelve acres of land and was the largest and most modern in Wales. It would provide employment for many Scarlets fans and players for years to come, continuing the relationship between the town and the production of steel and iron. However, the Old Castle Tinplate Works of The Steel Company of Wales would close in 1957. When it closed, 50 of the workforce were Italian and 70 women.

Llanelli player Handel Rogers was involved in what was at the time, the worst civil aviation disaster in the world. A plane he was on, along with 74 other Welsh rugby fans returning from seeing Wales clinch the Triple Crown in Ireland in 1950, crashed near Llandow airfield in the Vale of Glamorgan. Eighty people lost their lives, 75 passengers and five crew. Only three survived, including Handel Rogers and another Llanelli man, his brother-in-law, Gwyn Anthony. Handel would later go on to be President of the Welsh Rugby Union.

Moscow

Men of steel go behind the Iron Curtain

This is one of those strange but true chapters in the Llanelli story - one which is also not very well known for some reason. We're still in the 1950s and Russian leader Stalin has been dead for about four years. His successor, Khrushchev, wants to be seen as less dictatorial than Stalin. He wants the world to think that the Cold War has thawed a little and he wants to offer the hand of friendship to as many countries as he can. He decides the 6th World Festival of Youth and Students should be invited to his country. This happens, and in July

1957 34,000 young athletes from 130 countries descend on the Russian capital, Moscow. They are joined by 60,000 athletes from Russia itself.

The *New York Times* called the two week long event, a 'dizzying round of games, conferences, parties and carnivals.' Watching the Pathé news footage of the games certainly shows a mixture of the Llangollen International Eisteddfod and a major city carnival; a whole variety of sporting competitions, from hula hoops and track and field to motor bike racing and show jumping, all topped and tailed by Olympic style opening and

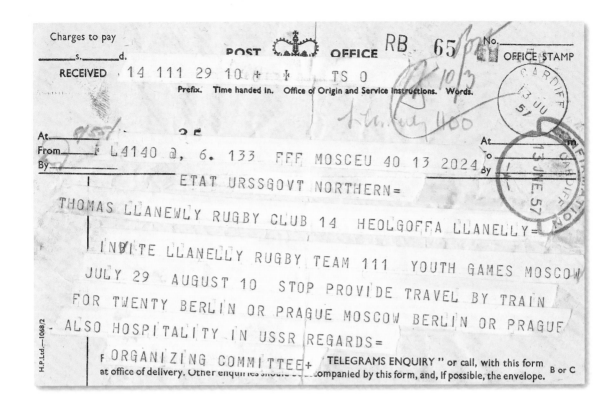

Caption (top): The original invitation telegram from Moscow.

closing ceremonies. Throw in a show of military power through the flypast of Russian planes, and the picture is complete.

Into this international extravaganza, enter Llanelli Rugby Club! Yes, it is hard to believe, but the club were invited to send a representation to the games in order to take part in the rugby competition. It's easy to underestimate the magnitude of the operation needed to make such a visit possible today, as we can jet anywhere at just about any time. Getting a whole team, plus officials, from Llanelli to Communist Bloc Eastern Europe would prove to be a very difficult and arduous task indeed.

Left: The Llanelli team outside Lenin University, Moscow. Standing, left to right: Glyndwr Jenkins, Howard Davies, Aubrey Gale, Henry Morgan, Bryan Thomas, John Brock, John Miles, Euros Bowen, Peter Davies, Terry Davies. Seated: Ray Williams, R. H. Williams, Handel Rogers, (Chairman) Wynne Evans, Geoff Howells, Cyril Davies. In front: Geraint Stephens, Mike Phillips, Carwyn James. Top: The original invitation telegram from Moscow.

The original invitation for Llanelli RFC to take part in the games was very late in arriving at Stradey — it had been sent to New South Wales in Australia!

To start with, they couldn't get enough money to get there. We've already read about the substantial investment plan the committee had embarked on in order to redevelop Stradey. There was no spare cash for a long trip, certainly not one of thousands of miles. Final confirmation that they could actually go didn't arrive until the 6 July 1957, and they would need to leave Llanelli on 21 July if they were to get there in time!

The Russian organisers had sent a telegram cable to club secretary Handel Rogers, saying that they could cover expenses from Berlin to Moscow, but not from Llanelli to Berlin. They would need £1000 for that journey and the club were in no position to cover it. Eventually, following much East-West negotiating, a compromise was reached and the Russians agreed to pay the club's expenses from London to Moscow. The club agreed to pitch up the money to take the team to the English capital.

In two weeks Handel Rogers had to sort out all the travel and visa arrangements for a full team of players and officials. The games were to open on 28 July, and they needed a week to get to Moscow. That long, long, long journey started on the platform of Llanelli Station and ended in the shadow of the Kremlin.

They caught the train to Dover, from which they caught a ferry across the channel. It was back on the train again across western Europe and into East Berlin. It's a journey one of the players remembers very well. Terry Davies was the team's full-back in those games.

'We arrived in East Berlin at night. We couldn't see much, apart from soldiers here and there. When we woke up the next morning, it was exactly like waking up in a war zone. The streets were clean enough, but there were buildings all around that were without roofs and glass. We stayed in the city for a few hours before leaving on the two day train journey to Moscow.'

The flight back from Moscow was the first time Handel Rogers had been on a plane since his involvement in the Llandow air disaster of 1950. In reply to an enquiry from one of his team-mates as to whether he was feeling ok on the flight his reply was, 'Whatever happens, at least I will be in good company.'

Above: Scarlets in front of the Kremlin.
Left: One of Handel Rogers' official passes on the journey.

Top: Llanelli players greeted with flowers by their hosts at Moscow Station; Ray Williams shows off his bouquet.
Above: The plane ticket home for one of the Llanelli players.
Right: Some players talk tactics, led by scrum-half Wynne Evans, with ball in hand.

Llanelli man Alan Oakley was the original contact between Games organisers and the club. He was at the Fifth World Youth Games in Warsaw in 1955 and kept in touch with those who organised British involvement in the games. They mentioned the need for a rugby team from Wales to be in the Moscow Games and, as time was too short to organize a full Welsh team to go, Llanelli were asked.

On the table the other side of the Scarlets were members of the Combined Oxford and Cambridge Rowing Team. Unfortunately they had been disqualified from their competition because their boat had capsized. At breakfast one morning, the Llanelli hooker Geraint Stephens, from Llandybie, decided that the rowing team's predicament needed to be addressed. On arrival at the table he turned to the Oxbridge table and greeted them with, 'Swimming today then, boys?' He started a cold war all on his own! The cravated and blazered Oxbridge boys fell silent and the atmosphere became very heavy indeed. Geraint followed up immediately. Noticing the caviar they had found and put on their morning toast, he turned to them again and asked inquisitively 'Well, where did you get the blackberry jam from, boys?' This broke the ice he'd formed a few minutes previously. Everyone laughed and international relations were restored. Every morning from then on the Oxbridge boys greeted Geraint Stephens with 'Good morning, Mr. Blackberry Jam man!'

The Romanians show off the cup they won by beating Llanelli in the final. That's the official line anyway!

When they eventually got there they stayed on the University Campus, just off Red Square. They could see that iconic square from their accommodation. Marquees had been erected on the college grounds and this is where the teams were fed. They had some free time after arriving, before playing Yugoslavia on their second day there.

They then played Czechoslovakia and beat them soundly by about thirty points. The next game was to be against France, but the French had seen Llanelli comprehensively beat their first two opponents and didn't want to face the ignominy of potentially suffering the same fate. Why? Because the other three teams in the competition were the national teams of their prospective countries and the up-till-then all-conquering Llanelli were of course 'only' a club side. The French stuck to their guns and didn't actually play Llanelli at all.

So, following a 35-9 victory against Czechoslovakia a 6-6 draw against Romania and the withdrawal of the French, Llanelli played the Romanians in the final. Twice! The first final was a draw, which the Russians insisted had to be replayed. Llanelli lost the second final 3-6. This extra game meant that Llanelli's had to fly home instead of catching trains and ferries. The trip really was a unique experience in the history of club rugby.

On the table next to the Llanelli team in the dining marquee were members of the Czechoslovakian team at the games. In their midst, the legendary Emile Zatopek who had broken all records in the Helsinki Olympic Games of 1952 by winning three gold medals — in the 5,000 metres, 10,000 metres and marathon. The marathon he won was the first he ever raced in his life. Scarlets players queued up to shake this great athlete's hand at breakfast time.

MOSCOW TAKEN BY STORM

eboard showing the llanelly's second game umania. Below the captain holds the t trophy and on Rhys Williams, the lanelly captain.

РУМЫНИЯ **6** ХЕНЕХИ **3**

They'll keep a welcome for Llanelly

By DEWI LEWIS

LLANELLY R.F.C. will very shortly receive written invitations to pay a return visit to Moscow, and also to play a Czechoslovakian side in Prague.

This was the news that a weary, but happy, party brought with them when they arrived at Blackbushe Airport, Hampshire, yesterday morning. Verbal invitations were extended in Moscow before the party left.

RUSSIAN WATCH

Civic welcome at Llanelly

WHEN the Llanelly rugby party arrived home last night the Mayor (Mr. Glyn Every) and Deputy Mayor (Mr. William Nurse) were waiting on the station platform to give them a civic welcome.

Scores of people thronged the station approach, and there were handshakes and congratulations for all the players, and the two officials who went with them, Mr. Handel Rogers, chairman, and Mr. Ron Harries, treasurer.

The local W.R.U. members, Mr. D. H. Thomas and members of the Llanelly committee were among the welcoming party.

"It's good to be home," said a beaming Mr. Rogers.

FOUR-YEAR-OLD ALAN THOMAS helps Ray Williams with his bag at Llanelly Station.

Reds rave about Scarlets

By DEWI LEWIS

LLANELLY rugby team arrived home from Moscow yesterday—the most feted, kissed, and bouquet-battered Welshmen who ever punted a ball.

And the Rumanians, whom Llanelly played twice in the Moscow international youth festival? They apologised for the "incidents" in the first match.

Hospitality

The players, still dazed by the

Before they boarded the plane the team had to promise to try to go back again—and to visit Czechoslovakia.

Official written invitations are expected soon from Moscow and Prague.

The team were unanimous in their praise of the Rumanians, to whom they lost the youth festival cup on the replay.

crowds would come up to us and shout with smiling faces—"Peace and friendship."

Moscow officials were "desperately keen" on Llanelly visiting them again and the Czechs had also made an approach, probably for a game at Prague, he said.

"It has been said that they'll be a good team in a couple of years, but they're good now," commented Peter Davies.

Before the start of the second

Some of the many headllnes heralding the success of the trip.

The Stradey Swinging Sixties
1960-1969

If the Sixties brought about changes to the way we live generally, then the decade certainly saw some changes in Llanelli Rugby Club. The Fifties introduced advances at the Stradey ground that would change the way the fans saw the game. Now, before the Sixties stopped swinging there would be changes in the actual game those fans would see from their new vantage points. It would become more organised, the structures would be different. One of the stars of the era, the legendary full-back from Hendy, Terry Price, described period as being when the club *'...settled down from being a Barbarian type side to becoming a well organised team.'*

But before all that would happen, and just like any other decade, a whole new breed of stars would be nurtured on the nursery slopes of Stradey. Whoever they would turn out to be, they would all play in a more illuminated way than their predecessors. Floodlights welcomed the dawn of a new decade at Stradey.

As the Sixties reached their terrible twos, in walked another player who'd started his rugby with the rivals over the bridge, Swansea. Norman Gale had won his Welsh cap, but had failed to secure a regular place as the Welsh hooker. That was a hard task – the man carrying that particular baton at the time was the great Billy Meredith. When he made his move, Norman said that the biggest impression made on him was the 'special closeness of

feeling' that was at the club and particularly at Stradey on match day.

He was one of the fifteen that faced the mighty All Blacks in 1963, but more of that in a later chapter. Contrary to popular belief, the already mentioned Terry Price didn't make his debut for Llanelli against the mighty New Zealanders. It is true he was still a schoolboy – in the sixth form at Llanelli Boys Grammar School –when he first pulled on the Scarlet jersey. But that was a few days before facing the All Blacks. His first game was in another fixture that is part of Llanelli heritage, the Boxing Day game against London Welsh. There was no one prouder that debut day for Terry than his grandfather – none other than Dai Hiddlestone, a former Scarlets player and captain of the club in 1919-1920. Terry had to ask his headmaster's permission to play for Llanelli, which was duly granted. But he also had to battle against a little opposition from the Welsh Secondary Schools organisation, especially when they learned that Terry was to play against New Zealand. They weren't too pleased that a schoolboy was to face such a power as the All Blacks. But whatever the objections, Terry played against them, another Welsh schoolboy thrown in at the deep-end of world rugby.

Captain of Llanelli on the day they took on New Zealand was Marlston Morgan. He proudly takes his place in the Llanelli story for not only the number of times he played for his

club – 465, a remarkable achievement in itself – but also for the fact that he played the full 80 minutes in all of those games! That's the equivalent of nearly twenty six days of the full twenty four hours playing rugby! Respect!

The Llanelli team that took on New Zealand in '63 contained many players who were the cornerstones of the team's building throughout the Sixties. Some have been mentioned already. Here's another one: Delme Thomas. He had just joined the Scarlets from St. Clears Youth – a team formed by Llanelli favourite, Howard 'Ash' Davies. Delme joined the Scarlets in 1960 and his second game for them – on 12 September 1960 against the Irish Wolfhounds – was on his eighteenth birthday. That very same day there was a little boy in Mynyddygarreg who was celebrating his ninth birthday, a certain Ray Gravell.

Top: Nearly all the players on the pitch within touching distance. Things have changed! Above: Marlston Morgan, who played the full 80 minutes in every one of his 465 games for Llanelli!

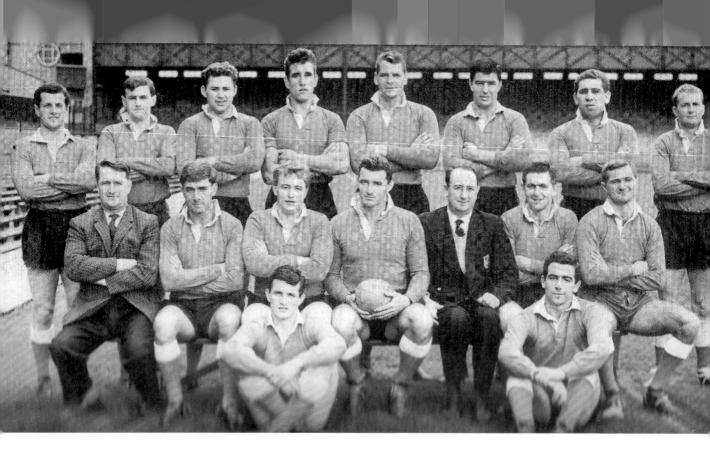

One player who didn't face the All Blacks was D. Ken Jones, the centre who had his first cap for Wales the year before in 1962. He was yet another who played his first game for the Scarlets while he was still in school, in his case Gwendraeth Grammar School. This was in 1960 and he was a member of the team who clinched the Snelling Sevens trophy for Llanelli for the first time ever that year. He went on to win 14 caps for Wales and six caps for the British and Irish Lions on two tours, scoring three tries for the Lions.

Llanelli captain on the day they clinched the Snelling Sevens was Onllwyn Brace, the mercurial scrum-half who played for Wales. His link with Llanelli, being a boy from the wrong side of the bridge, was that his brother John had played for the club in the 1940s. This meant that little Onllwyn was dragged to Llanelli to watch big brother play. Lucky for Llanelli! When he hung his boots up he went on to become Head of Sport for BBC Wales, succeeding Cliff Morgan

– who also turned out for the Scarlets once, believe it or not. More of this on the next page.

Onto the foundations set by such players in the early part of the decade, stepped some youngsters who would set the international rugby world alight in that decade and the next. Names such as Bennett, Quinnell and John. Say no more. Maybe the club didn't grab many honours in the Sixties, but so much of what was to follow can be traced back to the work done in this decade.

Barry John first played for Llanelli on 4 January 1964, and he went on to play 83 games for the club. That first game was during the school holidays as he was still in school at Gwendraeth Grammar School. Derek Quinnell first played for the club in 1964, the year the first youth side was formed at the club and where the young Derek first took his place. Phil Bennett first played in 1966 against the old enemy Swansea. Barry Llewelyn first played in 1966 as well. Four young players who the

Above: A fresh faced Barry John, before he was king.

Left: Llanelli 1962-1963. Standing (left to right): Brian Davies, Colin Elliot, Marlston Morgan, Delme Thomas, Tony Macdonald, John Warlow, Norman Gale, John Elgar Williams. Seated: Arthur Davies (Secretary), Gwyn Robins, Barrie Jackson, Bryan Thomas, (captain), Elvet Jones (Chairman), Dennis Thomas, Robert Morgan. In front: Stuart Davies, Freddie Bevan.

All Blacks would come to know all about in the early years of the Seventies.

In 1965, a nineteen-year-old Stuart Gallagher also joined the club. He played in the victory against the Wallabies in '67 and was then appointed the club's youngest ever captain. Andy Hill and Gareth Jenkins were two other names written in the club's players list in the Sixties, Gareth being the first Llanelli player to captain Wales Youth. All of these played their part in making Llanelli the force it was to become in the following decade.

One factor that links these players, and, many more over the years, is the link that they forge between Llanelli Rugby Club, the surrounding villages and the wider area.

Cliff Morgan played his one game for Llanelli in bizarre circumstances. According to folklore, he was at the train station at Newport, on his way to London where he was due to compère a concert. When he got on the train he landed in the middle of the Llanelli rugby team on their way to play London Wasps. But they were a man short. Carwyn James had missed the train because of some last minute teacher duties at Llandovery College. Cliff Morgan was asked on the train to take Carwyn's place and a few hours later he pulled on a Scarlets jersey. However, Cliff Morgan's name does appear in the match day programme!

Llanelli went behind the Iron Curtain once more in the Sixties. A trip was arranged to East Berlin where they played an Army team at the famous Spandau Prison! They had one very prominent spectator watching — well, it's not actually known for a fact, but it's not beyond the bounds of possibility. A prisoner at Spandau at the time was none other than Rudolf Hess, the Deputy Führer to Hitler, found guilty of atrocious war crimes and imprisoned for life.

𝕷lanelly 𝕽ugby 𝕱ootbal

SEASON 1964—1965

Front Row : Mr. GARETH HUMPHREYS (Hon. Treasurer), DENNIS THOMAS, MARLSTON MORGAN,
NOMAN GALE (Captain), Councillor W. J. THOMAS (President), JOHN LELEU, ROBERT

Middle Row : Mr. TYSSUL JONES (Assistant Trainer), GARETH THOMAS, ROY EVANS, GERALD,
JOHN JAMES, MORTON HOWELLS, HUGH HARRIES, CEDRIC JONES, Mr. W. TU

Back Row : Mr. GLAN JONES (Trainer), Mr. PETER REES, Mr. KEN JONES (Vice-Chairman) Dr. E. N
DELME THOMAS, Mr. GETHIN HUGHES, JOHN JOHN, P.C. STEVE JONES.

Clb

This legacy has been mentioned already, right back in the formative days, but as the club approached its centenary, it still held true. This is something that struck one of the Sixties stars on his arrival at the club from outside the area. Onllwyn Brace, referring to his years as club captain (1959-1961), said that what impressed him most was 'the very real contribution that the local areas around Llanelli made to the club.'

The big change at the club was to come as the decade was beginning to draw to its close. But that deserves a chapter all of its own.

Gerald Davies played for the Scarlets in the 1963-1964 season the first of nine games before going east!

Llanelli won the Floodlight Alliance Trophy for six years in succession at the end of the Sixties and into the Seventies. In one of these cup matches, in 1968 against Cross Keys, they scored 23 tries!

Clive John made his debut for the Scarlets as a scrum-half to his brother Barry against Rosslyn Park in 1966.

When schoolboy Terry Price faced the mighty All Blacks at Stradey in 1963, he was in no way intimidated by the opposition. In fact, he tackled the fearsome Waka Nathan, known as the Black Panther, so hard the New Zealand flanker broke his jaw.

Delme Thomas
Hero of the era

A fitting way to react to having been chosen for the Lions before you've played for your country! Delme 1966.

Until he was twelve years old, the hero of this era had no interest in rugby. The team he followed was the Swans and he'd pass Stradey often on the way to watch the likes of Ivor Allchurch and brothers Mel and John Charles. They were his heroes. But a new teacher's arrival at his secondary school introduced a new game to the boys, one which captured Delme Thomas' imagination, leading him to swap the round ball for the oval one. The teacher who first introduced rugby to St. Clears Secondary School – there wasn't even a rugby pitch there – was Howard 'Ash' Davies. He soon saw potential in the young Delme from Bancyfelin and introduced him not only to schools rugby but, in time, the youth rugby set-up as well.

It was also Howard who took Delme on to the next level after that. Having been asked if he felt like going for a trial with Llanelli, the unassuming Delme said that he thought his next step was to play for the Quins or the Athletic in Carmarthen and that he was too young to go to Llanelli. Howard listened carefully and then told Delme that he had booked him in to a trial with Llanelli anyway and he would pick him up and take him to Stradey himself. Thank goodness for teachers with vision!

At the time Llanelli were looking for a replacement for the great R. H. Williams who had hung up his boots. Some still thought Delme was too young and too small to fill the gap left by R. H.. There was no fitness coaching as such at the club at the time, so Delme's answer was to join the YMCA in Carmarthen and do his own weight training, trying to bulk himself up a bit.

It worked, and soon Delme settled in to the second row and by 1963, three years after joining the Scarlets, he was facing the All Blacks and marking the mighty Colin Meads. Three years later he was chosen for his first British Lions tour before he gained his first cap for Wales. He toured New Zealand and Australia, a long five month tour. Luckily for him his employers, The Electricity Board, gave him time off on full pay. He then won his first Welsh cap in that same year of 1966, against Australia in December. Two others who won their first caps that day were Barry John and Gerald Davies. Gerald wore the number 12 on his back – he wouldn't be moved to the wing until later in the decade. Terry Price also played in that match.

In 1968 Delme was called up for another Lions tour, this time to South Africa. He was the only Llanelli player on that tour. He didn't have a long run of appearances for his country, due to injury and tough opposition from Brian Thomas and Brian Price. By the end of the Sixties he had only played seven times for Wales, but he had toured twice with the British Lions and had served his club for a whole decade.

His finest hour, in fact his finest hours, were still to come. But the experience gained throughout the Sixties was a major factor in the decision taken by Maestro Carwyn James to turn to Delme when the club needed a leader to take on the All Blacks.

Oh no, we don't want coaches!

What did The British and Irish Lions have in common with international schoolboys in the Sixties? They would have been prepared for their matches by a man – and it would have been most definitely only been a man – known as a coach. A familiar enough idea today, but back in the day, a coach was a very rare animal.

In fact, if you played for your club, there was no coach. The Welsh national team didn't even have a coach right up to the mid-Sixties. There was coaching of course, there always has been. There were protests back in the 1890s that Welsh teams, Llanelli among them, practised for games and planned for them as well. How dare they?! Some, from outside the country, thought this to be outrageous and bordering on cheating!

But a pattern formed early on whereby all teams would be coached, and by the time we reach the 1960s it was a well-established tradition that coaching would be done by the captain. The hierarchy of the WRU thought that this was the best way. As late as 1964 this is what their President, Nathan Rocyn-Jones had to say, *'...the game was essentially played for enjoyment and that too much emphasis could be placed on technical and tactical skill.'*

They soon changed their stance and the first Welsh National Coach was appointed. He was David Nash and he took his place in 1967, the same year Ray Williams was appointed as Wales' first Coaching Organiser. In 1968 Clive Rowlands took over from Dai Nash as Wales

coach. Things were changing and moving forward. Rugby was getting serious.

But not at the clubs it wasn't. They were the last to see that they needed a coach. Dai Nash sums up the attitude of clubs to coaching, quoting the most representative attitude he'd heard himself:

'Oh no we don't want coaching, no need to coach clubs... Oh we've never had coaching, you know, we all pick it up, we're all natural players you know; oh no you'll stifle flair, no we don't want coaching'.

But things had to change. The clubs would have to follow the country. This inevitably came about as a result of a hundreds of committee meetings – it is Wales after all. What came out of these thousands of hours of talking was the decision that clubs have to have coaches.

The Llanelli committee was as ready to grasp this innovation as they were to develop the Stradey ground in the previous decade. In fact, they had taken some steps towards preparing players for matches before all that. They had come across Tom Hudson, the fitness man for the Swans at the Vetch and a former athlete. His arrival was soon followed by the appointment in 1967 of the first coach at Llanelli, the same year as Nash took over at Wales and Ray Williams started as Coaching Organiser. Llanelli had caught on to the coaching revolution very early on.

That's the history of how and why Llanelli got their first coach, something which made a huge difference to attitudes and approaches to the

Above: The man who went on to lead the rampant Lions in New Zealand.

Carwyn James would often turn up to train the Scarlets straight from lecturing at Trinity College. He would stand on the touchline in his suit and rugby boots on his feet, the bottom of his suit trousers tucked in to his socks. If he ran along the touchline, everyone could hear the box of matches rattling in his pocket.

The meeting to bring Tom Hudson to the club was held in the *Western Mail* office in Swansea. The club's then Chairman, Peter Rees, was there as was Glyn Walters, the man behind the public address microphone at Stradey who worked in that office in Swansea.

In the early days of coaching, the famous Tanner Bank, where hundreds of fans stood on match days, would be used for training. At that time it was a mound of rubble made up from the debris of old World War Two air raid shelters. Players would run up and down it and forwards would push each other up the bank — an early scrummaging machine!

Ieuan Evans' father was known as Ianto Red because he was one of the leading Communists in the Amman Valley, itself an important centre for Communism in South Wales.

Left: Ieuan Evans and Carwyn James. Right: Guess which one's the coach?

game itself. Now back to the club and how all this impacted on Llanelli RFC.

'This was an important phase in Llanelli's history.' That's how Stuart Gallacher sums up the 1967-1968 season. He goes further: 'The pre-season training was the hardest I remember in twelve years of first team rugby.' Things were definitely changing and the players were feeling it.

Llanelli's first proper coach, as we understand the word now, was Ieuan Evans. He had been appointed coach of the Welsh Youth team way back in 1962. Wales youth were the first to initiate the squad system in Welsh rugby, so Llanelli had a forward thinking man in charge. Systems were set up, tactics were discussed. The captain in that all important '67 season, Norman Gale, was not in charge of team performance any more.

Ieuan Evans set the foundations for what was to be a very successful period in Llanelli rugby, as did fitness guru Tom Hudson. He was then at Swansea University, but had previously been a pentathlete at the 1956 Olympic Games. He came to Llanelli and completely changed the way players prepared for games. Players recall, with a mixture of pain and fondness,

his regime of going for a run from Stradey to Burry Port and back. Andy Hill, the try machine on the wing for Llanelli, sums up Hudson's contribution.

'Most of his emphasis was on pre-season training and conditioning. In my own case, he changed my play completely, improving my fitness, attitude and pace. Two seasons after joining Llanelli, I took up athletics and joined Swansea Harriers as well as playing rugby.'

Ieuan Evans was replaced in 1969 by a man called Carwyn James. Quite simply, things would never be the same at Llanelli after his arrival. He was a House Master at Llandovery College at the time, responsible for continuing the success that college had always enjoyed in British schools rugby. He was also in charge of cricket at the College. The then Llanelli Chairman, Peter Rees, went to Llandovery to ask Carwyn if he would be the Llanelli Coach. Over a cup of tea and some cakes in Carwyn's study, he agreed. At about the same time he left Llandovery to be a lecturer in Trinity College, Carmarthen.

One of the first things Carwyn would have been told about after starting his new job with Llanelli was that they were to face South Africa.

That gave him a dilemma. He was strongly opposed to apartheid, the system in South Africa that segregated white people and black people. This carried on into sport as well and no black people would be allowed to play in a team of whites. Some countries boycotted South African sport for this reason and Carwyn had huge sympathy for this stance. His compromise for the Llanelli v South Africa game was to prepare the team but then refuse to watch the game himself in protest. Some say he went home, but the more likely account is that he stayed in the dressing room, listening to the game on the radio. Principle and duty were both served.

On the pitch it was a great game which Llanelli nearly won, losing in the end by just one point. Stuart Gallacher remembers Llanelli's equivalent to the Barbarians' 'that try'. *'Who could forget that Alan Richards try involving ten players holding the ball? I remember walking back from the South African try-line and seeing Springboks all around the field in complete disarray.'*

Later on that year, Carwyn was successful in applying for the role of coach for the British and Irish Lions tour of New Zealand the following year, 1971. He hadn't coached his country at that time and had only been in Llanelli for about eighteen months. That series proved to be an historical one with the Lions winning their first ever Testseries in New Zealand. The year after, well, 9-3 says it all. Then, there followed the run of Welsh Cup wins under Carwyn's guidance.

That chat over a cup of tea and cake in a Llandovery study, paid dividends beyond the expectation of even the most forward thinking committee.

All Blacks, Cups and Carwyn

1970-1979

So the Scarlets entered the Seventies with a narrow defeat against the Springboks, with a new system to play under and with a new coach. They would end that decade having achieved remarkable success that reverberated throughout the world of rugby. There's no doubt that Carwyn James moved things along very quickly once he got there, something which is evident in two very clear ways.

Firstly, once it was known that Llanelli were to play the All Blacks, he wanted to prepare for that game in his way. That would have been in 1971, the year before the game. Delme Thomas, who was on the infamous Lions tour that year, remembers Carwyn telling him out there that he would be facing these All Blacks on home soil very soon. Once back from that Lions tour, Carwyn wanted to be in control of the preparations for his club to play the same opposition. He asked the committee if he would be allowed to have the final say in choosing the team to play against New Zealand. The committee's pioneering decision for this new decade was to allow him that freedom.

The second indication that things moved quickly at the club at the start of the Seventies is something that Derek Quinnell has noted.

'Incredibly, looking at the South Africa game in January 1970 and the All Blacks game in October '72, within that short space, our side had changed enormously. Only two players played in both games, and that's quite incredible really. That was me and Hefin Jenkins. Phil Bennett and Delme were around at that time of course, but weren't allowed to play for Llanelli against South Africa because they had been chosen to play for Wales against them that same week.'

Those words not only show how quickly things were moving, but how unaccustomed the players were for things to change so fast.

Before Llanelli were to take on the All Blacks in '72, they went on a pre-season tour to South Africa. Carwyn once again stood by his anti-apartheid stance and didn't travel with the party.

One player had made a big decision about his career before going on that tour. Delme Thomas had decided that he was going to retire from the game. That was the announcement he would make after touching down back home and, sure enough, an announcement was made: that Delme was to be captain for the forthcoming season! It was he who would lead his team against the All Blacks.

STRADEY PARK
(PARC - Y - STRADE) LLANELLI

Boxing Day, Dec. 26, 1970

LLANELLI

V.

LONDON
WELSH

KICK-OFF 3.15 P.M.

Official Programme - One Shilling

WELSH RUGBY UNION

CUP FINAL

LLANELLI v CARDIFF

National Stadium
Cardiff Arms Park

Kick Off 3.00 p.m.

Saturday
28th. April 1973

Programme

The Cup Kings enjoy the celebrations and the trophies!

Delme was told about the decision to ask him to be captain on the plane on the way back from South Africa and it was enough to make him postpone his retirement – and lucky that it was, for him and everybody else in the rugby world!

Selection for the big game then was to be in the hands of Carwyn James, his assistant Norman Gale and now Delme Thomas as captain. Carwyn referred to them collectively as 'We Three'.

The game, on 31 October 1972, understandably has a chapter of its own. But that whole season was significant in another way in that it was deemed to be the centenary of the club. Yet, as you will have already read, the club wasn't actually formed until 1875, so there seems to have been a little bit of a mix-up with the centenary idea. But it was certainly announced way before the All Blacks game, not added on after the victory to make it seem more special. However, whatever the reason behind it, and

whatever facts have been confirmed since, you will still read and hear quite a lot about the All Blacks victory taking place in the centenary year.

You can't beat the 1972-1973 season for the sheer number of official events that were held. There was a full calendar of centenary events to start with and then, of course, a full run of celebration events following 'that victory'. It wasn't a good year to talk about the number of hot dinners you'd had as the Scarlets could probably double it. The culmination of all this festivity was a banquet on the pitch at Stradey, which took place under two large red and white marquees erected especially for the event. Llanelli had more star sporting guests back and fore to the town to speak at official functions that year than a whole series of This is Your Life or guests of Jonathan Ross. Guests of honour at this banquet for 650 included world renowned opera star Sir Geraint Evans, actor Clifford Evans,

Sir David Davies, Lord Alun Chalfont and Llanelli boy the Rt. Hon. Sir F. Elwyn Jones Q.C, the former Attorney General and the man whom Ty Elwyn is named after today. More importantly, his brother Idris played for Llanelli and Wales. Rugby royalty was represented by the likes of Ivor Jones, the King of Forwards, who had captained Llanelli for nine seasons.

Amid all the fanfares, clinking of glasses and the elation at beating the All Blacks, it's easy to forget – in fact most people have – that Llanelli also beat the Barbarians that year. That was an official Centenary Celebration game which Llanelli won 33-17. Andy Hill, Roger Davies (2), Roy Bergiers and Barry Llewelyn scoring tries for Llanelli, with Benny kicking the rest of the points. That victory would have been the headline story of that season, had not the 'other game' happened. The Baa Baas fielded 12 full internationals, including names such as Slattery, Burton, Cotton and Telfer. Twelve of the Llanelli players on the pitch that September midweek evening would play a month later against New Zealand.

Three who didn't play were wing J. J. Williams, flanker Tom David and scrum-half Ray 'Chico' Hopkins. These were the three transfers – the men that Carwyn wanted to bring in to Llanelli from other clubs to complete the squad to face the All Blacks. They came from Bridgend, Pontypridd and Maesteg respectively.

The Seventies at Stradey will always be remembered for the run of Welsh Challenge Cup victories the team enjoyed – a competition described as the most fiercely competitive in world club rugby. No doubt at the time it was. They lost the first ever final, against Neath in 1972 – yes they did lose something that year! But they soon made up for it, winning the Cup in 1973, 1974, 1975 and 1976. In these wins against Cardiff, Aberavon (twice), and Swansea they scored 73 points and conceded only 27. To date, the club has won the Welsh Cup, in all its various guises, twelve times.

This might come as no surprise, but after beating the Barbarians, the All Blacks and winning the Welsh Cup for the first time, the

Following the success of the Lions in 1971, Carwyn James and Delme Thomas were invited to open a new petrol station in Llanelli.

team were taken on a holiday. Albeit a rugby-playing holiday, but they were allowed to enjoy Canada's beauty as well as play a few games. That tour caused a considerable stir in Welsh rugby circles because, for the first time, wives and girlfriends were allowed to go as well. Quite revolutionary in those days, a major cultural earthquake! There were a few rumblings amongst the Llanelli players as to why partners were allowed to go, and there was certainly a great deal of banter and leg-pulling by members of every other club in South Wales! But coach Carwyn had insisted that this was to be because he felt that the partners had been as much a part of the team's outstanding season as their men on the pitch. Carwyn, again, ahead of his time.

Llanelli players played their part, of course, in the astounding Welsh success of the Golden Era Seventies. Phil Bennett, Delme Thomas, Derek Quinnell, J. J. Williams, Ray Gravell, Tom David and Roy Bergiers were not only Welsh caps but British Lions as well. Seven British Lions from one club in one decade. Little wonder that

Llanelli in this era were called the Manchester United of rugby.

But let's spare a thought for players who were both outstanding and loyal for the club in such a triumphant era but who didn't get their Welsh caps. Andy Hill, Selwyn Williams, Tony Crocker, Roy Thomas, Gareth Jenkins and Hefin Jenkins. In today's game they would have been capped, as many wore the Welsh jersey but, unfortunately for them, against teams you didn't earn a cap for in those days.

Left: Another Cup lifted. A definite Seventies habit. On that day in September 1977, Llanelli beat the Royal Regiment of Wales 41 -12.
Above: Prince Charles honoured by an invite to Stradey Park – and he met the players!

1975 Llanelli team photo.

Standing: Roy Thomas, Tom David. Barry Llywelyn, Allan James, Phil May, Roger Powell, Hefin Jenkins, Tony Crocker.

Seated: Ray Gravell, Andy Hill, Phil Bennett, Roy Bergiers, J.J. Williams.

Front: Keri Coslett, Bernard Thomas, Selwyn Williams.

Far left, Norman Gale.

2nd right, Carwyn James.

3rd right, Ever popular physio, Bert Peel.

Above: The Quinnell patriarch takes the field for Wales. Derek then begat Scott, Craig and Gavin. Right: Grav powers through the Romanian defence at the Arms Park... and through club opposition back home. This time it's against Bridgend.

What an excuse to include the famous Cliff Morgan commentary on the Baa Baas' try against the 1973 All Blacks. Three Llanelli players had a hand in the try:

'Kirkpatrick to Williams. This is great stuff... Phil Bennett covering... chased by Alistair Scown. Brilliant! Oh, that's brilliant! John Williams, Brian Williams, Pullin, John Dawes. Great dummy! David, Tom David, the half-way line. Brilliant by Quinnell. This is Gareth Edwards. A dramatic start. What a score!'

Rugby writer for *The Observer* and former Swansea player, Clem Thomas said this of the Llanelli v South Africa game in 1970: *'It drained the emotion by its turbulence, its physical contact and above all by the exhilaration induced by the style and spirit of a truly superb game of rugby.'*

The flowers at the end of the 1972–1973 banquet were red geraniums.

Scarlet greats R. H. Williams and Howard 'Ash' Davies were invited to give inspirational talks to the Llanelli players as part of their preparation for the 1973 Cup Final against Cardiff.

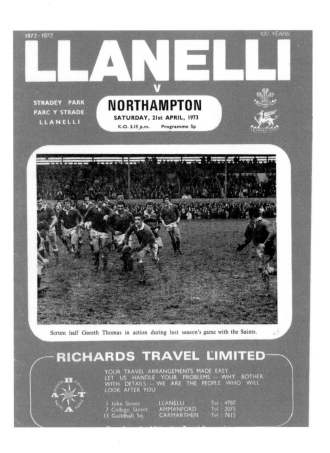

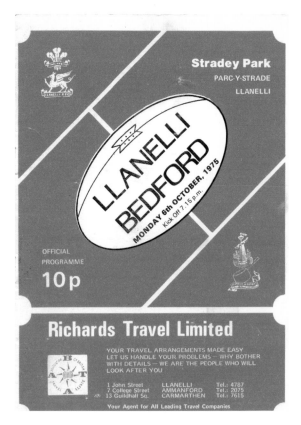

LLANELLI
Scarlet

37 – 17

15	ROGER DAVIES 4 4	Cefnwr	Full Back
14	ANDY HILL/CLIVE REES 4	Asgell Dde	Right Wing
13	ROY BERGIERS *W 4	Canolwr De	Right Centre
12	BERNARD THOMAS	Canolwr Chwith	Left Centre
11	RAY GRAVELLE	Asgell Chwith	Left Wing
10	PHIL BENNETT *W 3 2 4 2 4 2 2 2	Maswr	Outside-half
9	SELWYN WILLIAMS	Mewnwr	Inside-half
1	ADRIAN EVANS	Y Rheng Flaen	Prop
2	ROY THOMAS	Bachwr	Hooker
3	TONY CROCKER	Y Rheng Flaen	Prop
4	DELME THOMAS *W	Clo	Lock
5	DEREK QUINNELL *W	Clo	Lock
6	GARETH JENKINS	Blaenasgell	Wing Forward
8	HEFIN JENKINS	Wythwr	No. 8
7	BARRY LLEWELYN *W 4	Blaenasgell	Wing Forward

BARBARIANS
Black and White

37 – 17

(Rosslyn Park)	**RAY CODD**	15 2 3
(Bedford) *S	**BILLY STEEL**	14
(Ebbw Vale) *S	**ARTHUR LEWIS**	13
(Coventry) *E	**GEOFF EVANS**	12 4
(Loughborough) *S	**LEWIS DICK**	11 4
(Hawick) *S	**COLIN TELFER**	10
(Gordonians) *S	**IAN McCRAE**	9 4
(Loughborough) *E	**FRAN COTTON**	1
(Harlequins)	**DAVID BARRY**	2
(Gloucester) *E	**MIKE BURTON**	3
(Northampton) *E	**JOHN LARTER**	4
(Richmond) *E	**CHRIS RALSTON**	5
(Neath)	**DAVID MORRIS**	6
(Rosslyn Park) *E	**TONY RIPLEY**	8
(Blackrock Coll.) *I	**FERGUS SLATTERY**	7

Rheolwr/Referee: Mr. MEIRION JOSEPH, Swansea

*Internationals: (England) (Ireland) (Scotland) (Wales)

Touch Judges: G. A. Ferguson (London Society) Meirion Davies (Llanelli)

10 JULIE 1972

TRANSVAAL

VERSUS

LLANELLI

ELLISPARK ·········· JOHANNESBURG
AMPTELIKE PROGRAM   30c

In the match programme for the Transvaal versus Llanelli game on the 1972 tour, their President refers to Llanelli as the most famous club team in the world.

Above: The programme became very much a part of the match day experience in this era and fans began to take a biro to matches to record the players and scorers.

Phil Bennett
Hero of the era

Another tough one. Especially after naming six British Lions a few sentences ago. But it has to go to one man – Benny. He captained his club for six seasons, from 1973-1974 to 1978-1979. In this period Llanelli won two Welsh Cups and two Welsh Club Championships. That is remarkable enough in itself. But that's not the only reason he's the hero of the era. There's so much more.

As a youngster, Phil was a talented sportsman whose ability drew the attention of some football teams. Fortunately for the Stradey faithful he chose the oval shaped ball not the round one. He was offered scholarship to go to Llandovery College by none other than the College's rugby master, Carwyn James. But he turned that down when tragedy struck the Bennett family and his father had a nasty accident in the steelworks. Benny was still in school, and had to leave at 15 in order to bring some income in to the household. No prizes

for guessing that he started work in one of the town's foundries.

There are so many 'what ifs' already in his story! But what we do know, of course, is what actually happened. He started playing rugby for Felinfoel and won seven Welsh Youth caps from his village team before joining Llanelli. He made his debut for the Scarlets against Swansea in 1966, a game he says he doesn't remember much about because he doesn't remember games he lost!

Three years later he pulled on the Welsh jersey for the first time and made rugby history by becoming the first player to come on as a substitute in an international game. That was in the Stade Olympique in Paris in an 8-8 draw against France. Gerald Davies was still in the centre in those days and Phil came on instead of him – but played on the wing! The story goes that he didn't touch the ball at all in his international debut.

He went on to win 29 caps for Wales and within the ten year period he played for his country and the sixteen years he played for Llanelli, he kept churning out ground-breaking statistics that would have Carol Vorderman's head in a spin. In addition to captaining his club for six seasons, he played over 400 games for them, scoring over 2,500 points. For Wales he had the record for the most number of points scored in an international career, a total of 166. That's scoring nearly six points every time he played for Wales. He shared the record of most points in one Championship season, 38, with Roger Hosen, Tony Ward and Steve Fenwick.

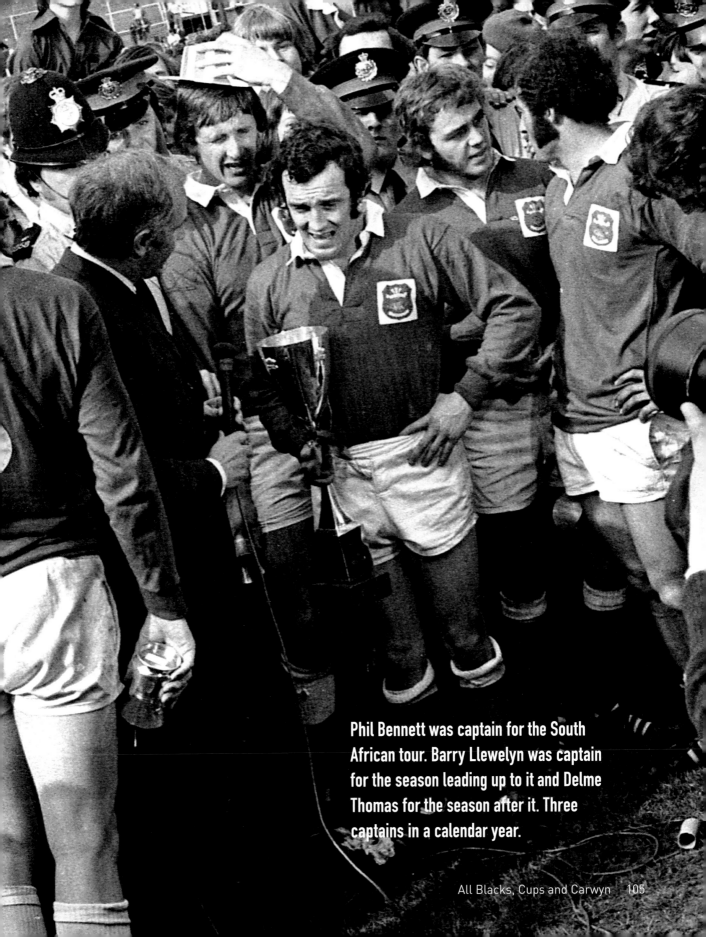

Phil Bennett was captain for the South African tour. Barry Llewelyn was captain for the season leading up to it and Delme Thomas for the season after it. Three captains in a calendar year.

He captained Wales eight times and led his country to victory in seven of those eight games, securing two Triple Crowns and one Grand Slam. He shares what was then the record number of appearances for a half-back pairing for their country, partnering Gareth Edwards 25 times. He was a member of the undefeated Lions in South Africa in 1974, scoring 26 points in the four Test matches. And to cap it all, he was given the honour of being the captain of the Lions on their tour to New Zealand in 1977, scoring 112 points in 14 games. Finally, on top of all that, his try against Scotland in 1977 was voted the greatest ever Five or Six Nations try by BBC Scrum V viewers. Amazing statistics!

He was, however, famously deemed to be the third choice outside-half in Wales at one time with John Bevan and David Richards being chosen ahead of him for the Welsh team of 1975-1976. Lesser mortals would have let their heads drop at such decision but Benny showed his reaction where it matters most, on the pitch, continuing to shine for his club. Luck played a part too, both other fly-halves suffered injuries and had to pull out of the England game, allowing Benny back in. He played in the other games in that campaign too, scoring 38 points and equalling Keith Jarrett's record of 19 points in one game – the one against Ireland. Justice of the truly poetic kind!

We'll give the last word to *The Daily Telegraph*, in an article in 2009 accompanying the announcement of their Greatest Lions XV, with Benny chosen ahead of Barry John.

A fitness fanatic, Bennett was 30 years ahead of his time, a model professional despite the absence of a wage packet. He would have graced the modern game, filled huge stadia and unpicked the tightest of in-your-face defences. He would have mocked them and made those on the touchline tear up their coaching manuals.

In November 2005 Phil Bennett
was admitted into the International
Rugby Hall of Fame and, in 2007,
to the Welsh Sports Hall of Fame.

Who Beat the All Blacks?

The greatest day in the club's history. A simple enough statement to make. But before we look at the events surrounding 31 October 1972, let's sound a cautionary tale. The response to that famous victory hasn't always been positive. There has been a time in the Scarlets' story since then when looking back to '72 has been a negative thing. There has been a tendency to live in that day and not to move on from it. The secret of making the most of success is to enjoy it and celebrate it and then knowing how to move on from it. That process had faltered and staggered, but is now on the right balance, using yesterday to move on to tomorrow.

Touring teams had been coming to these shores for a very long time before 1972. But they didn't come half as often as they do today. A visit from one of the Southern Hemisphere sides was a very special occasion, looked forward to and prepared for years in advance. It was always going to be an exciting event.

The All Blacks' visit to Llanelli in 1972 had an extra edge to it however. The British Lions, under coach Carwyn, had beaten them in a Test series for the first time the year before. They were hurting; the sporting pride of this rugby nation had been seriously battered and they had revenge in mind. Carwyn now faced them as coach of his club. British Lion Delme Thomas was team captain. British Lion Derek Quinnell was in the Llanelli team. Add to these talented men, the undoubted qualities of Carwyn's assistant coach, Norman Gale. His input was as influential as the Maestro himself.

We wouldn't fill many pages analysing the tactics of the game. It was a brutal affair. The ball wasn't in play for much more than ten minutes. There was only one try scored, a conversion and two penalties. But it was a try, a conversion and a penalty to Llanelli and only a penalty to New Zealand. The result was oh, so sweet! As was the impact the game had on places far beyond the Loughor Bridge. There are so many stories around that game to do with the event, the occasion, as much as with the eighty minutes on the pitch.

The players all had day jobs to start with. That's easy enough to forget in this professional era. They all had to negotiate time off to be free to play. They all obviously succeeded, but not all in the same way. Roy Bergiers was a teacher then, in Carmarthen, and he was given permission to have the day off but without pay. Some of his fellow teachers, standing on the terraces watching him score the crucial opening try for Llanelli, had the afternoon off to watch the game with pay!

Above and right: A fan's delight to be treasured – a first day cover envelope to mark the visit of the All Blacks in 1972... and inside, the bumper match day programme. A special memento of an extraordinary day.

STRADEY PARK 1872 - 1972
PARC Y STRADE

LLANELLI

LLANELLI

NEW
ZEALAND

31st. OCTOBER 1972

THE NEW ZEALAND RUGBY TOURING TEAM 1972-73

T. J. (Trevor) Morris .	B. (Bevan) Holmes
J. F. (Joe) Karam .	I. A. (Ian) Kirkpatrick
B. G. (Bryan) Williams .	A. I. (Alistair) Scown
D. A. (Duncan) Hales .	K. W. (Ken) Stewart
G. B. (Grant) Batty .	A. J. (Alex) Wyllie
G. R. (George) Skudder .	M. (Ian) Eliason
B. (Bruce) Robertson .	A. (Andy) Haden .
I. A. (Ian) Hurst .	H. H. (Hamish) Macdonald .
R. M. (Mike) Parkinson .	P. J. (Peter) Whiting
M. (Mark) Sayers .	G. J. (Graham) Whiting .
R. E. (Bob) Burgess .	J. (Jeff) Matheson
I. N. (Ian) Stevens .	K. (Keith) Murdoch
S. M. (Sid) Going .	K. K. (Kent) Lambert
G. L. (Lindsay) Colling .	R. W. (Tane) Norton .
A. R. (Alan) Sutherland .	B. A. (Ron) Urlich .

16. – VISIT OF NEW ZEALAND RUGBY TOURING TEAM
TO LLANELLI ON 31ST OCTOBER 1972

An application submitted on behalf of the Manual Workers for leave of absence on the afternoon of Tuesday, the 31st October to enable those wishing to attend the Rugby Match between Llanelli R.F.C. and the New Zealand Rugby Tourists be granted subject to essential services being maintained and to any other exigencies of the services administered by the Council; that this privilege be granted also to the Craftsmen and Staff.

**Top: A page from inside the programme.
Above: Some made official applications
for time off to see the game. A lot didn't!**

THE LLANELLI RUGBY TEAM THAT DEFEATED THE ALL BLACKS AT STRADEY PARK ON TUESDAY, OCTOBER 31st, 1972, BY 9pts. TO 3pts.

Derek Quinnell has played against the All Blacks four times and won four times — in three different positions and with three different clubs! A remarkable record in world rugby.

'Brilliant Delme speech had me in tears' That was one of the headlines in the *Western Mail* the day after the match, as Phil Bennett sums up the whole squad's reaction to the talk captain Delme Thomas gave them before the game. It was one of those team talks that will go down in rugby folklore as the gentle giant shared that he would swap all his honours, including winning a Test series with the Lions, if the mighty All Blacks could be felled in his own backyard. It was heartfelt, stirring emotion, calmly but sincerely delivered. It worked.

Gareth Jenkins, the day before the match, was called to do an urgent repair job on one of the massive ingot stopping gates in The Klondike, that sprawling steelworks which opened in the early days of the club and was owned by Duport in '72. He was working in a confined space on that Monday, in intense heat. He was perspiring so much his clothes were soaking. No regard for the fact he was to face the All Blacks the next day. His summing up of the game? 'From the kick-off, it was just brutality!'

Hooker Roy 'Shanto' Thomas used to collect cockles, sell coal, and own a fish shop before he arrived at the Velindre Steelworks, which is where he was in 1972. 'I remember it was pressure all the time' he recalls. The man under his armpit one side, Tony Crocker, worked for Morris Motors, then owned by British

Leyland but still called Morris Motors in the town. He remembers that the atmosphere at Stradey hit him when he walked on to the pitch, 'We showed a lot of courage to hold out and keep the lead we got in the first five minutes.'

The occupier of Shanto's armpit the other side was Barry Llewelyn. He was a teacher in Tenby who also had just opened a sports shop in Llanelli. He was given time off from school, with pay. His abiding memory is being kicked in the backside by tough New Zealand prop, Keith Murdoch, and the ref telling Barry to get up off the floor and stop wasting time!

Behind the front row, Delme Thomas was a linesman with the Electricity Board, climbing poles in all sorts of weather. He had instilled in his players what he had learned in '71, that the

worst thing you can do against the All Blacks is to let them come at you. 'You've got to go out to meet them first.'

Derek Quinnell, in the back row, was a rep for a British fertilizer company. He was aware of the psychology that had been instilled in them before the game, as much as the physicality. After it was all over, he said, 'It wasn't a nice place to be but it was an exciting place to be.'

Tom David worked for a subsidiary company of British Airways as a technician. 'It was a battle royal from the word go but we had the crowd with us. They played as much a part in that victory as we did on the pitch.'

Left and right: The victory inspired artists and poets alike. Above: One of the iconic photos of that day, shared the world over. Delme Thomas lifted up on high by exultant fans.

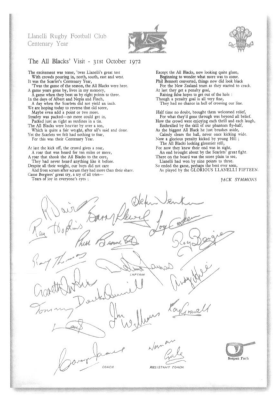

Llanelli Rugby Football Club
Centenary Year

The All Blacks' Visit - 31st October 1972

The excitement was tense, 'twas Llanelli's great test
  With crowds pouring in, north, south, east and west.
It was the Scarlets's Centenary Year,
  'Twas the game of the season, the All Blacks were here.
A game years gone by, lives in my memory,
  A game when they beat us by eight points to three.
In the days of Albert and Nepia and Finch,
  A day when the Scarlets did not yield an inch.
We are hoping today to reverse that old score,
  Maybe even add a point or two more.
Stradey was packed—no more could get in,
  Packed just as tight as sardines in a tin.
The All Blacks were heavier by over a ton,
  Which is quite a fair weight, after all's said and done.
Yet the Scarlets we felt had nothing to fear,
  For this was their Centenary Year.

At last the kick off, the crowd gives a roar,
  A roar that was heard for ten miles or more,
A roar that shook the All Blacks to the core,
  They had never heard anything like it before.
Despite all their weight, our boys did not care
  And from scrum after scrum they had more than their share.
Came Bergiers' great try, a try of all tries—
  Tears of joy in everyone's eyes ;

Except the All Blacks, now looking quite glum,
  Beginning to wonder what more was to come.
Phil Bennett converted, things now did look black
  For the New Zealand team as they started to crack.
At last they get a penalty goal,
  Raising false hopes to get out of the hole :
Though a penalty goal is all very fine,
  They had no chance in hell of crossing our line.

Half time no doubt, brought them welcomed relief,
  For what they'd gone through was beyond all belief.
How the crowd were enjoying each thrill and each laugh,
  Enthralled by the skill of our phantom fly-half,
As the biggest All Black bit just brushes aside,
  Calmly clears the ball, never once kicking wide.
Now a glorious penalty kicked by young Hill ;
  The All Blacks looking gloomier still,
For now they knew their end was in sight,
  An end brought about by the Scarlets' great fight.
There on the board was the score plain to see,
  Llanelli had won by nine points to three.
So ended the game, perhaps the best ever seen,
  As played by the GLORIOUS LLANELLI FIFTEEN.

JACK SYMMONS

CAPTAIN

COACH   ASSISTANT COACH

Sospan Fach

After the match a well-suited fan went up to Gareth Jenkins, full of praise and admiration. At the end of their chat, he gave Gareth a £10 note in order for him to buy steaks to put on his two severely blackened eyes. Having said his heartfelt thanks for such a kind gesture, steak was the last thing on Gareth's mind. The money he had been given was as much as a week's wage, so he used it to take a few more days off work to 'recover' from the match!

Later that evening, both teams and their officials were at the Ritz Ballroom in the middle of Llanelli town. Amongst the acts booked to entertain the rugby fraternity were entertainment duo Ryan and Ronnie, who went on to dominate light entertainment in Wales in both languages and have not been surpassed to this day. Some players actually remember them being there.

Hefin Jenkins was a student in the Glamorgan College of Technology, and we already know what Gareth Jenkins did. 'I don't remember a great deal of detail at all, it was all lost on the cut and thrust of the game itself.'

Scrum-half Ray 'Chico' Hopkins was a PR officer for Everwarm Homes, trying to persuade local authorities to use their central heating systems. He remembers the one that got away, 'I put a grubber kick through and my bloody ankle got tapped or I'm sure I would have scored in the corner!'

In the centre, Grav, the youngest player on the pitch, did the same job as Delme. He commented on Carwyn's decision to take Llanelli to see the All Blacks play Western Counties in Gloucester the week before, 'Looking back, I would be prepared to say that planning the trip that afternoon to the West of England was the greatest psychological aid that he gave us in all the preparations.'

On the wing, J. J. was a PE teacher, playing in what he described as 'my first big occasion ever.' Roger Davies the full-back was a student in Trinity College Carmarthen – 'I didn't think we had won the game until the final whistle had been blown, it was too dangerous to think it before then!'

Finally, on the other wing was Andy Hill. Following a short spell at The Klondike, he was a rent collector for Swansea Council in October 1972. Referring to his monster long range penalty that turned the score in to the famous 9–3, he said, 'I was so thrilled, I jumped into the air and straight into Tommy David's arms! I'd never done anything like that before or since!'

Most of these men were back in work on the Wednesday morning after the game and the late night celebrations. It was, literally, a different world. The following Saturday, they lost to Harlequins. There's no truth at all to the rumour that some players were still the worse for wear after the Tuesday before!

Left: Scorer of the only try of the game, Roy Bergiers proudly signs the wallpaper photo of the team to mark 40 years since the defeat of the All Blacks.
Right: A lasting memento, forged in a Llanelli foundry.

WELSH RUGBY

17½p • MANAGING EDITOR STUART WEAVING • JUNE, 1973

100 GLORIOUS YEARS

1872   1972

LLANELLI R·F·C

The team met at the Ashburnham Hotel in Pembrey beforehand and travelled in to Stradey by coach, with rows of bannered and scarved fans along the pavements cheering their heroes. It was just like a cup final procession — except this was rugby. Grav sat on the bus next to Delme, who had the tough job of calming down an excitable Grav even before they were anywhere near Stradey.

A few days after the game, the young, fledgling Max Boyce was on BBC Radio in Wales singing about the game in his famous song that talks of inspiration piped down from Felinfoel and of pubs being drunk dry. This was a major factor in widening the impact of the game beyond the Scarlets region.

Doris 'Where's the salad?' actress from *Gavin and Stacey*, Margaret John, who was also Mrs Hepplewhite in *High Hopes*, met her husband because of the match. They met when he returned to a mutual friend's house after watching the game in a pub in London. He was very impressed that Margaret knew who was playing and that she asked what the score was. They soon got married.

The Maestro behind the legendary Groggs, John Hughes, was at the match, along with his son, and the effect that one victory had on everyone made him rethink his whole business. Instead of concentrating on mythological figures as he had been, he thought it might be a good idea to concentrate on sculpting rugby figures. Delme's victorious double armed salute after being lifted shoulder high by fans was a very early piece.

Phil Bennett stands near a commemorative plaque still hanging on a pub wall in Llanelli.

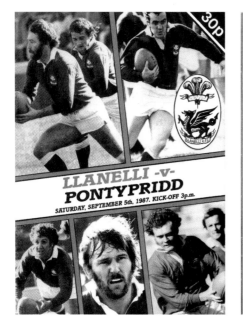

Rebuilding to be the Best in Britain

1980-1994

This is one of those periods that won't be remembered so much for club success as for brilliant individual players who set the Welsh rugby world alight. It was a difficult period of trying to move on from a golden era. But, having said that, right at the end of such an era for shining individuals, comes one of the best team seasons the club has ever enjoyed! So really, it's a mixed bag of an era which then ended with a fundamental change in the way that rugby was run, not just in Llanelli but throughout the world-wide rugby world.

But before saying hello to a new era, there were a lot of goodbyes. Two flying wings, who were veritable try-machines for the club, hung up their boots. Andy Hill and J. J. Williams were different types of players; one not recognised by his country despite scoring an astonishing 311 tries for his club. The other, scoring tries just as freely, was honoured by both Wales and the British Lions. Both played in the victory against the All Blacks. Andy Hill retired in 1979 having scored 2596 points for the club. A remarkable achievement for a loyal club man.

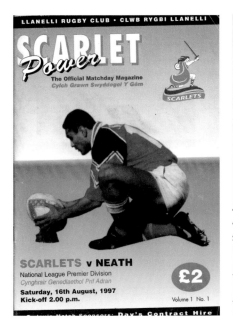

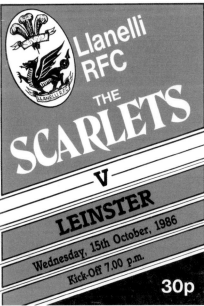

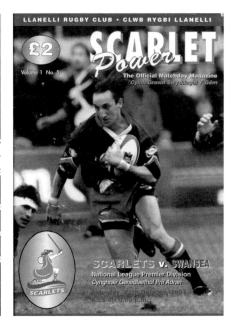

The following year, J. J. retired. He played thirty consecutive games for Wales and scored twelve tries in Five Nations Rugby playing on the wing, winning four consecutive Triple Crowns and two Grand Slams in the process. He enjoyed success with the Lions too, going on two tours – in 1974 to South Africa, and 1977 to New Zealand. On the 1974 Unbeatables tour he scored four tries in the Test series. He also scored six tries in one provincial match which equalled the Lions record at the time. When he hung up his boots he was the second highest try scorer in the history of British Lions rugby.

Phil Bennett went in the early Eighties too, having played in over 400 games for the club and scoring over two and a half thousand points. A few years later, in 1985, Ray Gravell had played his last game for the club. He played in 485 games and scored 120 tries. These four men between them played in well over a thousand games for Llanelli and contributed about seven thousand points.

It was definitely a time of rebuilding, but fortunately the start of the Eighties saw the appointment of two master builders to the club. In 1982, the coaching responsibilities were in

the hands of Gareth Jenkins and Allan Lewis. They enjoyed a long period of success, initially in putting together a team to replace the stars of the Seventies and then in securing trophies and one particular famous victory. But more of that later.

Gareth Jenkins first got involved with the club in 1967-1968, when, in his own words, he was an 'enthusiastic teenager.' He played for many years before an injury brought his career to a premature end. He was a tough flanker who took no prisoners in any of his 250 games for the club. He played two tests for a Wales XV against Japan in 1975 but caps weren't awarded for that fixture.

A similar fate saw the early end of Allan Lewis' career as well. He broke a leg while playing in the centre for Llanelli against Swansea, the treatment didn't work and that was the end of his playing days.

These two injured players made a formidable coaching team. They were heavily influenced by the Maestro, Carwyn James, in their approach to the way the game should be played. They also embodied a strong tradition in the Llanelli

story, emphasised more than once already –
that of the link between local clubs and the
team of the town. It wasn't only true of players.
Allan Lewis had cut his coaching teeth with
clubs such as Ammanford and Pontarddulais
while Gareth earned his spurs with his village
team, Furnace.

The first silverware came in 1985 with yet
another Welsh Cup, this time a 15-14 victory
against Cardiff. This was indeed an astonishing
achievement and will be remembered for the
boot of Gary Pearce, the leadership of Phil May
and the fingertips of Phil Davies. It has to be
said that other teams had passed the Scarlets
as the Seventies gave way to the Eighties as

others had learned from the Scarlets' way.
When the 1985 Cup Final came round, the
hot favourites were the team of the moment,
Cardiff. Ex-Scarlet Gareth Davies was the Blues
number 10 and his partner was Terry Holmes.
With the clock just crossing the full eighty
minutes, the capital team were ahead 14-12.
The ball came to number 10 Gary Pearce's
hands who was ten metres in from the touchline
and thirty metres from the posts. He aimed a
drop goal at the posts and it sailed through.
15-14 Llanelli! But the ref allowed the restart
and Gareth Davies had a chance to emulate his
opposite number. He fired a drop goal which
would have given them the lead and almost

certainly the cup. Big Llanelli number 8, Phil Davies, just got his finger-tips to the ball and deflect it enough for it not to go through the posts. The final whistle blew and the cup was Llanelli's! It was the start of a new era for the club – in Llanelli at least, the Seventies started again in 1985.

The cup was back at Stradey in 1988 following a 28-13 victory against Neath. Playing number 10 for Llanelli that day was a former apprentice painter and decorator called Jonathan Davies. He made a brief appearance at Llanelli in 1981 for a trial as a young schoolboy, but things didn't work out that day and he ended up joining Neath. No sooner was he back in Llanelli than he was playing against his former club in a Cup Final. And he shone! But it was his tactical kicking that made this a memorable game for him, rather than his running, as he masterminded a victory for Llanelli against firm favourites Neath. Not long after, 'Jiffy' was going north, joining Widnes in January 1989.

The cup was only away from Llanelli for two years and when it returned, it stayed there for three years in a row. Cup success in 1991, 1992 and 1993 restored Llanelli as the Cup Kings, the latter victory being their ninth cup success. They beat Pontypool, Swansea and Neath in their Nineties run.

The era ended then, with a triple dose of Scarlet Fever. It was the season in which Laurance Delaney played his 500th game for the club and Phil Davies his 250th. Eleven Scarlets were chosen to play for Wales that season and eight played in the same game against France. Everyone was once again sitting up and taking notice of what was happening down at Stradey. No wonder, they had plenty of reason to.

Coach Gareth Jenkins urged his players to push for immortality, just like his mentor Carwyn James had done before the '72 game. But the former Scarlets flanker carved out his own

Above: Coach Gareth Jenkins, a shrewd and passionate man. Left: The tale of two tens. Jonathan Davies and Phil Bennett.

niche of Llanelli history – winning the Heineken League, the Swalec Cup and beating world champions Australia. To cap all that, Llanelli's match programme was voted the best in the UK, taken to such heights by former club historian, Les Williams. Llanelli were understandably given the title the Best Team in the UK when the glorious 1992-1993 season came to an end. Rebuilding just doesn't get much better than that: from losing pillars of the team, the introduction of new coaches, and a poor decade for the Welsh National team – to being the best club in the land.

The success even reached the Mother of Parliaments on the bank of the Thames. An Early Day Motion was put before the members,

asking for Llanelli's success to be officially recognised. Not all of the 24 MPs who signed the motion were from Wales.

Llanelli Rugby Football Club

Session: 1992-93
Date tabled: 10.05.1993
Primary sponsor: Davies, Denzil
Sponsors: Total number of signatures: 24

That this House congratulates Llanelli R.F.C. on its remarkable achievement in the 1992-93 season when it won the Welsh League Championship and the Welsh Cup, as well as defeating the Australian touring team; notes that these triumphs were gained by playing stylish and open rugby in the highest tradition of rugby football; and records the tremendous contribution made to Llanelli rugby by its senior coach, Mr. Gareth Jenkins, a true gentleman of the game.

Neath MP Peter Hain officially suggested an amendment that should be added to the original Motion. It shows clearly that rugby banter was alive and well in the corridors of power as well as on the wet and windy terraces.

'...but further congratulates Neath R.F.C. on its excellent performance against Llanelli in the Swalec Cup Final in the face of hostile and dubious refereeing.'

Further afield, the biggest change at the close of this era was the final end of the sham amateurism of the game. Shamateurism was finally buried as the professional era became official. Players could be paid for their labour, officially now, with no need for brown envelopes or the surreptitious stuffing of notes into rugby boots. At last it was all above board, giving rightful recognition to those who put their boots on to put in a good shift on the pitch.

Above: A worthy victory parade around Llanelli town after beating the Wallabies and winning both Cup and Championship in 1992-1993. Phil Davies is rumoured to have sung Tina Turner's *Simply the Best* all the way around town! Right: Great Scott giving Gavin Henson a slap!

Before the 1988 Cup Final, Jonathan 'Jiffy' Davies had a card in the post. It was postmarked Neath. Thinking it was a best wishes card, he opened it expectantly. To his surprise, the card inside had a picture of a hangman's noose on it, with the letters RIP underneath. It was signed by the Neath squad. A bit of rugby banter that backfired as it did nothing more than spur Jiffy on to play a blinder against the loving card-senders.

The Eighties was a rare decade for Llanelli as two scrum-halves were capped for their country within a few years of each other. The club has not supplied Wales with many number 9s, but Mark Douglas and Jonathan Griffiths were both capped in the Eighties – Mark in 1984 and Jonathan in 1988-1989. Up until that point, only Handel Greville (1947), Wynne Evans (1958) and Onllwyn Brace (1956) had worn the Welsh and Scarlet number nine. Selwyn Williams and Dennis Thomas, two of the best scrum-halves the Scarlets ever had, were never capped.

Ieuan Evans
Hero of the era

Many players were brought into the Scarlets fold during this era. Some would be loyal club men who served the team faithfully, some would be unsung heroes, others would be stars for their country and a few would wear a Lions shirt. Jenkins and Lewis brought in Scott Quinnell, and Gareth Jenkins was the only Union club coach Scott played under. Rupert Henry St. John Barker Moon was another colourful addition to the Llanelli fold, a scrum-half who captained the team for three seasons in a row, from 1992 to 1995, and who scored 77 tries in his 272 games. Up front, policeman Phil Davies joined in 1982 and stayed for thirteen years, captaining the club for six seasons – no mean achievement. Phil May played in over five hundred games for Llanelli and was a hardworking, loyal club player. He eventually had his international recognition at the ripe old age of 31 against England at Twickenham in 1988. Phil could end his career as a Triple Crown winner. Just rewards indeed.

But the stand-out player (who crosses from this era in to the next, but we'll nominate him in this one) is Ieuan Evans. He scored a try after just 45 seconds in the Cup Final against Neath in '93, but he's the hero of the era for much more than that!

Ieuan started to play rugby at Queen Elizabeth Grammar School for Boys, Carmarthen in 1974. He first played for Llanelli when he was a nineteen-year-old geography student in Salford University in 1984, having already started to shine for Carmarthen Quins. He quickly settled at Llanelli and was soon one to set the fans alight with his electrifying running. He stayed at Llanelli until 1997.

The Welsh set-up soon noticed him and he gained his first cap for Wales in 1987 against France in Paris. He was lucky enough to be playing at a time when the master commentator Bill McLaren still had the microphone in his hands – McLaren dubbed him 'Merlin', likening him to a Welsh magician on the field.

He went on to win 72 caps, 71 of which came while he was at Llanelli and the 72nd while he was with Bath – against Italy at Stradey Park! He was the Welsh captain for 28 of those internationals – a record at the time and an achievement that earned him another nickname, Captain Cymru. He captained Wales to Five Nations victory in 1994. He was a British Lion three times, travelling to Australia in 1989, New Zealand in 1993 and South Africa in 1997. As a Lion, he made many more memorable contributions. He scored the series winning try in the final Test against Australia and scored four tries against the All Blacks – a rare achievement for any player and one which made him the top try scorer for the Lions on that tour.

He appeared in seven cup finals for his club, winning five of them. He scored many memorable tries for both club and country, scoring a total of 194 for his club.

- The one against England in 1993 when he completely outpaced Underwood and Webb to score and turn defeat into unlikely victory. He scored from a deft little chip ahead from none other than blind side flanker Emyr Lewis. This was No. 17 in *Wales Online's* 20 Greatest Tries in Championship History.

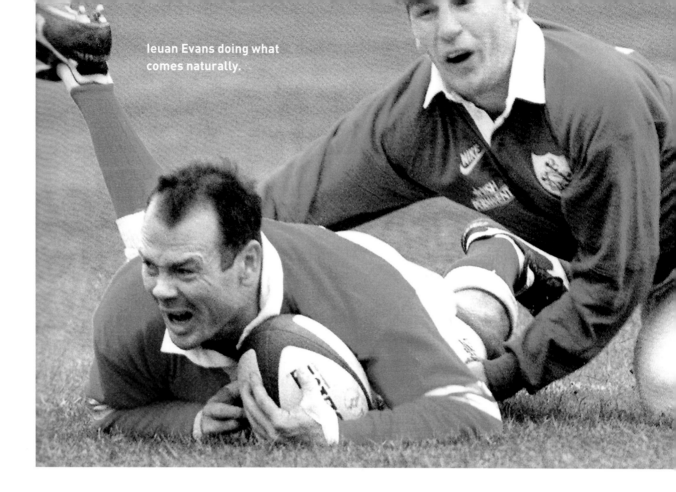

Ieuan Evans doing what comes naturally.

- The one for the Baa-Baas against Argentina in 1990. Phil Davies had a hand in this one.

- The one against Scotland in 1988, side stepping half the Scottish team to cross near the posts. This was No. 6 on the *Wales Online* list.

You've probably got your own favourite. He twice scored six tries in a game – against Merthyr in 1986 and against Maesteg in 1992, equalling a club record set by Alby Davies in 1902.

The fact he did so well in a decade that wasn't particularly successful for the Welsh set-up makes his achievements all the more noteworthy. As captain, he never failed to inspire his team-mates and led by try-scoring example.

In 2002 he was chosen as the Sportsman of the First 20 Years of S4C and in 2014 was installed in the IRB Hall of Fame.

Cardiff
Cambridge Blue and Black

15	P. Rees
14	G. Cordle
13	A.J. Donovan †
12	D. Evans
11	A.M. Hadley †
10	W.G. Davies †
9	T.D. Holmes (Captain) †
1	J. Whitefoot †
2	A.J. Phillips †
3	I. Eidman †
4	K. Edwards
5	R.L. Norster †
6	O. Golding
8	J.P. Scott †
7	G.J. Roberts †

Replacements
16 M. Carrington
17 C. Webber
18 S. Cannon
19 C. Collins
20 J. Souto
21 R. Lakin

Llanelli
Scarlet Jersey, White Shorts

15	M. Gravelle
14	P.I. Lewis †
13	N. Davies
12	P. Morgan †
11	I. Evans
10	G. Pearce †
9	J. Griffiths
1	L. Delaney
2	D. Fox
3	A. Buchanan
4	P. May (Captain)
5	R. Cornelius
6	A. Davies †
8	P.T. Davies †
7	D.F. Pickering †

Replacements
16 P. Hopkins
17 P. Fleming
18 K. Townley
19 R. Thomas
20 A. Griffiths
21 J. Cooper

15

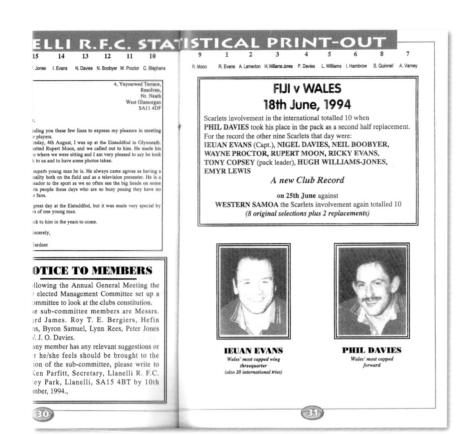

15   14   13   12   11   10   9   1   2   3   4   5   6   7

. Jones   I. Evans   N. Davies   N. Boobyer   W. Proctor   C. Stephens   R. Moon   R. Evans   A. Lamerton   H. Williams Jones   P. Davies   L. Williams   I. Hambrow   S. Quinnell   A. Varney

4, Ynysarwed Terrace,
Resolven,
Nr. Neath
West Glamorgan
SA11 4DF

,

nding you these few lines to express my pleasure in meeting
r players.

rsday, 4th August, I was up at the Eisteddfod in Glynneath.
otted Rupert Moon, and we called out to him. He made his
o where we were sitting and I am very pleased to say he took
k to us and to have some photos taken.

superb young man he is. He always came across as having a
nality both on the field and as a television presenter. He is a
sador to the sport as we so often see the big heads on some
ts people these days who are so busy posing they have no
e fans.

great day at the Eisteddfod, but it was made very special by
s of one young man.

k to him in the years to come.

incerely,

ardner

FIJI v WALES
18th June, 1994

Scarlets involvement in the international totalled 10 when
PHIL DAVIES took his place in the pack as a second half replacement.
For the record the other nine Scarlets that day were:
IEUAN EVANS (Capt.), **NIGEL DAVIES, NEIL BOOBYER,**
WAYNE PROCTOR, RUPERT MOON, RICKY EVANS,
TONY COPSEY (pack leader), **HUGH WILLIAMS-JONES,**
EMYR LEWIS

A new Club Record

on **25th June** against
WESTERN SAMOA the Scarlets involvement again totalled 10
(8 original selections plus 2 replacements)

IEUAN EVANS
*Wales' most capped wing
threequarter
(also 20 international tries)*

PHIL DAVIES
*Wales' most capped
forward*

OTICE TO MEMBERS

llowing the Annual General Meeting the
elected Management Committee set up a
ommittee to look at the clubs constitution.
e sub-committee members are Messrs.
rd James, Roy T. E. Bergiers, Hefin
ns, Byron Samuel, Lynn Rees, Peter Jones
. J. O. Davies.
any member has any relevant suggestions or
r he/she feels should be brought to the
ion of the sub-committee, please write to
Ken Parfitt, Secretary, Llanelli R. F.C.
ey Park, Llanelli, SA15 4BT by 10th
mber, 1994.,

30   31

Ricky and Phil making a bit of a potion in the South Seas

Welcome to Stradey Park
Croeso i Barc y Strade

OFFICIAL PROGRAMME   £1

HARP LAGER

Volume 1 Number 2

LLANELLI R.F.C.
Moseley
Date: Thursday, 1st September, 1994
Kick off: 7.15 p.m.

The 1990's gave us a Magnificent
Ten as ten Scarlets players pulled
on the red of Wales on their tour of
the South Sea Islands. A definite
legacy of the record breaking 1992-
1993 season for the club, proudly
noted in a match day programme.

Peter Morgan was chosen to tour South Africa with the British and Irish Lions in 1980. He was uncapped at the time and at 21, he was the youngest member of the squad. Ray Gravell and Derek Quinnell were also on that tour.

The team who won the league in 1992-1993, played 36 games in total, won 32, drew one, lost only three. They scored 136 tries in 22 league matches; Wayne Proctor and Ieuan Evans scoring twenty tries each. Champagne rugby indeed!

In 1992, the mischievous Mr Moon and the rest of the squad gave Ieuan Evans yet another nickname. They called him Mr Clean as, according to them, he hated getting dirty.

January 1983 saw the sudden death of Carwyn James, the legendary coach and broadcaster. He died on Monday, 10 January and Llanelli were to play Swansea two days later. There was talk of calling off the game but, instead, they decided to play the game, out of respect for him. Swansea were on an unbeaten run of 17 games but following a rousing team talk from Grav — you can just hear it now can't you? — the team honoured the Maestro with flowing rugby and a 16–9 victory. As the *Evening Post* said, '*Carwyn James would have approved. They didn't just take Swansea apart — they did it in style!*'

The Tanner Bank was demolished in 1990 in order to make way for the North Stand.

Many pre-'93 former Scarlets captains admit to having to play a trade union negotiator role on match days. One, who wishes to remain anonymous for fear of being nabbed by the rugby police, testifies to walking out at Stradey before a game to see how much of a crowd had gathered. If the ground was full, he would go to the treasurer to try and negotiate a few extra pounds for his players!

Phil Bennett played his final game at Stradey against Northampton. After the game, sitting in the dressing room, he reflected on the end of a glorious career: *'It was a terrible feeling, but then I looked around the room and thought of the great players and traditions that had gone before me and thought, 'Hell, be proud you have been part of the greatest club in the world'.*

LLANELLI
AUSTRALIA

STRADEY PARK
(Parc y Strade)
Llanelli

Tuesday
November 4th, 1975
Kick Off 2.30 p.m.

Souvenir Magazine
20p

STRADEY PARK
LLANELLY

AUSTRALIA

AUSTRALIA
v.
LLANELLY

December 10th

HARDS

half Gareth Thomas in action

Many came, many saw, many were conquered!

Llanelli have always taken their rugby to far away fields, right from those early days back in the century before last. They have also always welcomed rugby teams from foreign fields to Llanelli, again right from the very beginning. Welcoming international touring teams has been a proud part of the Scarlets tradition. Now however, it's a tradition that has come to an end as the way rugby is structured has changed. So we look back now on the visit of touring teams as a historical feature of the club's life, a look at the way things used to be. And it has to be said that such visits were not only enjoyable, they also used to be fairly successful for Llanelli.

Maoris

The first to venture from foreign lands to far away Llanelli were the Maoris of 1888. They played their very first game of their Welsh visit at Llanelli, but suffered a defeat. Llanelli won by a goal and five minors to five minors. There was a bit of extra edge to this game as Llanelli felt particularly aggrieved that only one of their members had been chosen to play for Wales. They felt this was nothing short of an insult as the local paper, *The Llanelly Mercury*, duly reported. They had to beat the Maoris then, and they did, thanks to a memorable drop goal by Harry Bowen. So there, Welsh selectors! Llanelli beat the Maori Army in 1919 and then beat the Maoris again in 1926 in a game called one of the most thrilling in the history of the club. There's nothing in the score to suggest as much as it finished 3-0 to Llanelli. But the fast attacking play of the Maoris was stopped in

its tracks by some ferocious Llanelli tackling, especially from Albert Jenkins and Tom Evans.

Australia

Australia were the first of the international powers that we would recognise today to be beaten by Llanelli. As we've already noted, this victory was immortalised in song as an amendment to the club anthem 'Sospan Fach.' The game itself was an 8-3 victory for the town team. That early success on the world rugby stage, according to the *Llanelly and County Guardian*, 'added another feather to

their already numerous plumes.' The way the pack played drew particular praise from all and sundry, with Tom Evans, hailed as the best forward playing in Wales at the time, scoring a try. The pride with which the match is reported in the papers is as clear as the print on the page. It's evident that this game affected the whole town, as did the 1972 All Blacks victory. Expectations were set, a tradition had begun. It was something worth singing about.

The Australians were back in 1927 in the shape of a New South Wales team. They soundly beat Llanelli, 24-14 in a game called one of the most remarkable ever seen at Stradey. The Scarlets and the Waratahs put on a superb display of rugby.

The second victory against the Australian national team came in 1967, the first victory for the Scarlets against a touring team for over forty years. It was a dour game to be honest, but it was set alight by a brilliant Barry John try right at the end and, of course, by the fact that Llanelli won. There were injuries all round as the negative brutal rugby took its toll. The points came from a penalty and a conversion by full-back Dennis Lewis, and a try and a drop goal from Barry John. After the match, Llanelli chairman Elvet Jones summed it up: 'I do not like this type of rugby, but it still goes down in the record books as a Llanelli victory.' A refreshingly honest appraisal.

Victory number three against the Wallabies came in that record-breaking season of 1992-1993. But before that there was that epic drawn game against them in 1975. Llanelli, with the roar of 1972 only just having died down, were up for the men from Down Under. With twelve minutes left on the clock Llanelli were 28-16 ahead. Following a penalty and a converted try the Wallabies were within three points as the eighty minutes approached. They were awarded a penalty, which was successfully converted,

and it ended all square; a draw snatched from the jaws of both victory and defeat!

Revenge, then, was very sweet in 1993. The odds didn't look good for the Scarlets. The Aussies arrived as World Champions, having won the previous World Cup. But Llanelli were enjoying a remarkable season and they had a good record against the Aussies. Was it possible again?

The game started as it was to go on. Heavy tackle after heavy tackle from the Scarlets players floored Aussies who were intent on running the ball. The ball did, they didn't. Amongst the forwards, Phil Davies, Emyr Lewis and Mark Perego were on fire. Only one try was scored, an absolute gem started off by Colin Stephens. He threw a few dummies, and offloaded to Ieuan Evans who was try-line bound at hundred miles an hour. With the eighty minutes approaching, the Wallabies were a point ahead. Another agonising defeat by one point looked likely for Llanelli, and the spirit of South Africa 1970 loomed large. But Colin Stephens paid no attention to history. He lined up for a drop goal, and when he hit the ball the crowd groaned. The ball stayed low, very low. It wouldn't have the legs to go over the bar. But it did, just. Llanelli 10 Australia 9. Fired by his first success, Stephens had just enough seconds left to do exactly the same again! Llanelli 13 Australia 9. 'Who beat the Wallabies?' was ringing around Stradey once more.

South Africa

Llanelli have welcomed and beaten teams from so many countries, but the South Africans are the only ones who they have only welcomed. The beating just hasn't happened. They first came here in the Edwardian days of 1906. Over 20,000 packed in to Stradey to see the match which was held on 29 December, in the bleak mid-winter. The straw wasn't cleared from the ground until less than an hour before kick-off,

Llanelly Football Team v South Africans 1906.

Llanelli v Australia 1908.

Top: Llanelly v
Australia 1951-1952.
Right: Four survivors
of the Llanelli team
that beat the Maoris
in 1926 watched the
Llanelli v Maoris
game in 1982.
From left to right:
Ernie Finch, Ivor
Jones, Rees Thomas
and Emrys Griffiths.

although they had more clearing time than they thought as the South Africans didn't arrive at Stradey until after the kick-off time. That didn't put them off their stride though and they won the game 16-3.

They were back six years later in front of what was called a 'record crowd'. Llanelli played really well and put the South Africans off their stride. It was a hard fought battle with Llanelli losing by the narrowest possible margin, 7-8.

It was nearly 20 years before the 'Boks were back. 24 November 1931 saw another close encounter, with captain Ivor Jones leading a fierce Llanelli fight, especially in the first half. But the South Africans were too strong and won 9-0. It was another twenty years before Llanelli welcomed a South African team, almost to the day. On 23 October 1951, the fourth Springboks side arrived at Stradey, this time to face Ossie Williams' team which included R. H. Williams. And as with most of the previous performances against touring teams, it was the Llanelli forwards who led the attack. They won the vast majority of the thirty-seven scrums, no mean feat against a Test team from South Africa. But the Boks had a solid defence and ended up winning 20-11. The Llanelli points came from a Des Jones try, converted by Lewis Jones; a Les Phillips drop goal and a monster Lewis Jones penalty.

There wasn't such a long wait this time before they were back. 13 December 1960 saw a rather one-sided game which Llanelli lost 21-0. Llanelli only had four internationals in their team that day – full-back Terry Davies, wing Ray Williams, centre Denis Evans and scrum-half and captain, Onllwyn Brace. Terry Davies' performance will be remembered for stopping famous crash tackling South African Francois Roux in his tracks. Davies tackled him and sent the man, renowned for having left a trail of opponents sprawling in his wake, bouncing into touch '... like a rubber bullet', as one paper said.

Individual players played well, but it wasn't the team performance needed to beat such strong opponents.

Nine years later they were back again, this time for that famous narrow defeat already mentioned in passing. It was Carwyn James' first match as coach against touring opposition and his approach to the match has already been told. Suffice to say that it was another loss to the South Africans, again by one point.

There's one more visit to tell of, with the Sprinkboks returning in the 1990s, 1994 to be exact. It was another loss, 30-12, and the last time the South Africans played on tour at Llanelli.

New Zealand

The South Africans had been to Llanelli twice before the mighty All Blacks made their first appearance in the town in 1924. They have been here eight times in all, but we only seem to remember the one victory! To be fair, Llanelli have come close to beating them a few times.

The 1924 game was dubbed one of the finest games ever played at Stradey and both teams were congratulated for the way they played the game. Llanelli had already beaten the New Zealand Maoris (1888-1889) and the New Zealand Army (1919). So the All Blacks arrived with a point to prove. They did, and won 8-3. Another point noted in a newspaper report was the attendance. Not the actual figure but:

Considering the unemployment, the attendance exceeded expectations.

The role of rugby in the life of the town, for richer or poorer, was evident once again.

After another visit from the Maoris in 1926, the All Blacks were back in 1935 to face Ivor Jones' Llanelli. Llanelli lost, 16-8.

Ieuan Evans, try scorer in Llanelli's victory against the Wallabies in 1992–1993 season.

Soon after the end of World War Two some of the Anzac boys were at Stradey, as Llanelli again took on the New Zealand Army, losing 16-8. Future Welsh international and club chairman Peter Rees played in this game. Eight years later, in the Coronation and Everest-conquering year of 1953, the All Blacks returned, this time running out winners by 17 points to 3. Match reports were quick to point out that the visitors scored 11 of their 17 points after Llanelli left wing Ron Thomas had been injured. The score, it was said, flattered the visitors.

Ten years later, they were back. Llanelli's team had familiar names on the team sheet – Terry Price, Norman Gale, Delme Thomas and Marlston Morgan, to name but a few. New Zealand also had some big names – Whineray, Nathan and a certain Colin Meads to name but a few. The game will be remembered as the day

a Llanelli Grammar School boy took on the All Blacks as Terry Price shone that day.

The Scarlets went in 8-3 up at half time, much to everyone's surprise – well, everyone outside Llanelli that is. The game ended in a 22-8 victory for New Zealand. *The Llanelli Star* adds, with shades of 1953, that

The tourists scored their last sixteen points when Llanelli had only thirteen men.

Beverly Davies, the outside-half, was concussed at the start of the second half and taken off and wing Robert Morgan had limped his way through most of the game. It's credit to Llanelli that, when it was fifteen against fifteen, they were ahead.

We all remember the next visit, already dealt with in a previous chapter. Eight years later, the All Blacks were back once more and this time it was the baby of the '72 game, Grav, who

'After the game, there was obvious euphoria, but also a sense of relief that we hadn't let the name of the Scarlets down.' Ieuan Evans

led his team against the familiar enemy. Again, Llanelli led at half time, 10-3, through a Bennett penalty, a Mark Jones try and a Martin Gravelle drop goal. But New Zealand ended on top of a game that most commentators said should have ended in a draw, winning 16-10.

This game will be remembered for the bizarre way in which it ended. It was a game full of the usual rough and tumble between these two teams. Paul Ringer especially was given extra attention by the All Black forwards and the ref, Scotsman Alan Hosie, had to speak to both captains and many players during the eighty minutes. As the game drew to a close, All Blacks lock Graham Higginson trampled on a Llanelli player. The ref looked as if he was going to send Higginson off, but Grav and Phil Bennett intervened and, in what was an extremely unusual gesture, they tried to persuade the ref not to send him off.

No-one expected this, least of all the ref. His response was to blow the final whistle, a good few minutes early, and both teams walked off in silence, with no-one quite sure what was going on. Had Higginson been sent off? Why was the whistle blown early? Post-match, the ref said that it was full time and that he had only cautioned Higginson. Grav and Benny state that the ref was definitely going to send him off. So why did they intervene? It was all down to diplomacy. There had been many incidents in games between the All Blacks and Llanelli, and other Welsh clubs and the Welsh team as well. Remember Murdoch being sent home from the 1972 tour, the acting ability of Haden in the lineout in 1978 and Tom David and Grant Batty in 'that' game in '73? These are just a few. Grav and Benny didn't want the 1980 game to be another on such a blacklist. They didn't want the special relationship between Llanelli and New Zealand to be marred by a sending off. So they intervened. Llanelli lost the game, but politically, they had the victory.

Before the decade was over, they were back. 1989 saw another defeat, 11-0, the All Blacks scoring two tries and a penalty. There was serious doubt before the match as to whether it should be played at all because the weather was so bad. It was decided to carry on with the game, but driving wind and rain made playing almost impossible. New Zealand captain Wayne Shelford said he had never played in such bad conditions.

The weather wasn't the problem on their next visit. It was the result. How good it would be to forget an 81-3 trouncing on the day Llanelli were Cullen-ed! Full-back Christian Cullen scored four tries for the All Blacks in a scintillating display. They were a team who put 130 points past Wales, Ireland and England, before drawing the second Test against England 26-26.

For all the match analysis, what the post-mortems really showed was that it was 'the end of touring teams playing against club sides.' The Southern Hemisphere players had been professional for a long time, and they came here to take on players with day jobs. All of a sudden it wasn't a level playing field. A long,

Right (top): 1926 Llanelli team v Maoris. Standing (left to right) Oswald Morgan (chairman) Ewan Thomas, Harry Morris, Rees Thomas, Watcyn Thomas, Bobby Evans, Fred Harries, Alf Parker, Emrys Griffiths, Ned Roberts (touch judge). Seated: Sid Hay, Tom Evans, Ivor Jones (captain) Albert Jenkins, Ernie Finch. In front: Cyril Jenkins, Dai John.

Right (bottom): 1935-1936 Llanelli team v New Zealand. Left to right: Capt. Bryn S Evans (Chairman) T. H. Phillips (referee) Gwyn Bayliss, Emrys Davies, Ray Smith, Jim Lang, W. Gwyn Lewis, W. R. J. Jones, Dai John, W. H. Clement, Elvet Jones, Will Williams, J. L. G. Morgan, Bryn Evans, Emrys Evans, Ron Harries, Ivor Jones (captain).

THE SCARLETS

30p

-V-

QUEENSLAND

Tuesday, 21st January, 1986. Kick-Off 7.00 p.m.

LLANELLI RUGBY FOOTBA
Stradey Park, L

LLANELLI v. QUE

TUESDAY, JANUARY 21,
Kick-Off 7.30 p.m.

Stand Ticket (Entrance B)
TOWN END

No 391

Ho

respected tradition of international teams taking on club sides had, sadly, come to an end.

Other visitors

Llanelli have welcomed touring teams from many other countries, including Canada, Tonga, Fiji, Western Samoa and Romania. In 1908 they made their first foray abroad, playing Racing Club in Paris. They have since been abroad many times on tour, to places such as Germany, Italy, Jersey, South Africa, Canada, Spain, Australia, Fiji, USA, Hungary and Slovenia.

Finally, who can forget that come-back of all come-backs in the game against Fiji in 1985? The South Sea Islanders took a commanding 28 points to nil lead. By half time, Llanelli were back to only 28-10 and they eventually ran out winners of the game 31-28! Remarkable!

Right: Scarlets v Racing Metro 107 years after the men from Llanelli first played the team from the French capital. Jake Ball takes two of them on at Parc y Scarlets in 2015.

In the Maori match report, the *Llanelli Mercury* refers to the Llanelli team as the Scarlet Runners. The *Llanelly and County Guardian* used the same term in their report on the 1912 South Africa game.

The 1888 Maoris arrived on the newspaper train in to Llanelli and stayed at the Salutation Hotel. When they left, a huge crowd were at the station to see them on their way singing 'Hen Wlad fy Nhadau' as they left.

During the game against New Zealand in 1935, C. R. Mansel Lewis, the Squire of Stradey and club president, had to ask the police to move some fans from the roof of the stand. The structure had groaned a few times too many for his comfort when the fans on the roof got a little too excited about some passages of play by Llanelli.

By the 1935 game against New Zealand, the popular Tanner Bank had suffered from inflation – the price to go in was raised from a tanner to a bob. If you don't know someone who can translate that to new money, a tanner was two and a half pence and a bob was five pence. The name, however, didn't change to the Bob Bank. Another Welsh team, with a different shaped ball, grabbed that name for one of their terraces.

WALES v ITALY

Stradey Park
LLANELLI

Saturday 7th February 1998

WRU
CYMRU

CYMRU v YR EIDAL

Parc Y Strade
LLANELLI

Dydd Sadwrn 7fed Chwefror 1998

The Lloyds TSB International **TSB**

Kick-off 6.00pm
Official Programme £2.00

Cychwyn 6 o'r gloch
Rhaglen Swyddogol £2.00

Reebok

Stradey Park—Parc-y-Strade
Llanelli

LLANELLI

The All Blacks at Stradey, 1935.

NEW ZEALAND

Tuesday, 21st October, 1980
Kick-off 2.30 p.m.

Official Programme 40p

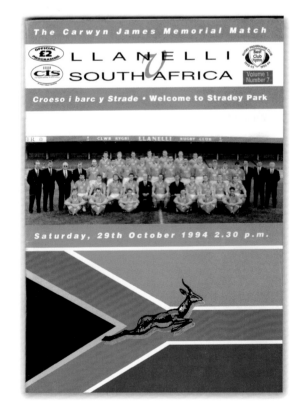

The Carwyn James Memorial Match

£2
OFFICIAL PROGRAMME

CIS

LLANELLI
v
SOUTH AFRICA

Volume 1
Number 7

Croeso i barc y Strade • Welcome to Stradey Park

CLWB RYGBI LLANELLI RUGBY CLUB

Saturday, 29th October 1994 2.30 p.m.

THE CARWYN JAMES MEMORIAL MATCH

LLANELLI RUGBY FOOTBALL CLUB

Todays Match Sponsor
DYFED STEELS

Volume 3
Number 8

CLWB RYGBI LLANELLI

LLANELLI
v
WESTERN
SAMOA

Stradey Park, Llanelli
Saturday, 23rd November, 1996
Kick off: 2.30 p.m.

Official Programme: £1

There was a special article in the match programme for the Llanelli Fiji game in 1995 written by none other than broadcasting elder statesman, Trevor McDonald (he hadn't been knighted at the time.) Here are some of the things he said:

Few requests have given me greater pleasure than to be asked to write something for Llanelli Rugby Football Club's programme… Long, long before I ever went anywhere near Llanelli, or for that matter, knew where it was in Wales, I had the opportunity as a much younger man in the West Indies to savour the enormous reputation of this great Rugby Club.

Trevor McDonald
News at Ten – Stradey Park

Few requests have given me greater pleasure than to be asked to write something for Llanelli Rugby Football Club's programme on the occasion of the Club's hosing of the international match against Fiji.

Long, long before I ever went anywhere near Llanelli, or for that matter knew where it was in Wales, I had the opportunity as a much younger man in the West Indies to savour the enormous reputation of this great Rugby Club. It formed part of a much wider appreciation of what, even in less celebrated times, I still describe as the glory of Welsh Rugby. In the time honoured manner of all-knowing non experts the world over, I have always characterised that glory as the beauty of the open game. To that I can add, flair, grace and style. Those are the qualities of Welsh Rugby which attracted me all those years ago, and they are the identical ones I reflect on now, whenever Wales run out onto the field.

I was never a player at any level, although some Rugby was played in Trinidad, my native land. My lack of enthusiasm had something to do with the climate. However much we hail those brilliantly warm days in temperate climates, I felt that Rugby was never made for tropical climes. I could never countenance running in to slide in a try on those harsh, unyielding West Indian grounds, baked hard in never changing seasons, by an unforgiving sun. Rugby is a game for autumn or winter, in countries where the ground can be wet and soggy and where the leaves blaze forth a change of colour before they float away in that wonderfully soft, pale afternoon light.

And yet the Rugby which has made clubs like Llanelli so internationally famous across the years did have a certain relation to at least one aspect of West Indian sport. West Indians play CRICKET with the same FLAIR. Its an uncompromisingly open game, with all the mistakes such a mode of play is heir to, but never, never less than entertaining. It is my view that the Fijians do the same. Not for them all the highly technical brilliance at the back, but an emphasis on marauding forwards, always looking to run the ball, always desperate to see it put over for a try.

How marvellous then that they should be playing in these famous surroundings, where the welcome is always warm and considerate and where the Rugby can be beautiful and explosive. May it be one to remember. I'll be there with you all in spirit, recalling as I chastise myself for missing the game, those unforgettable matches in South Africa.

TREVOR McDONALD
News at Ten

9

New home, new name, same heritage

1995-2015

And so to more recent times, and to the era that has probably seen the greatest amount of change in the club's history. Pretty much everything changed over this twenty year period. Professionalism had already come in through the front door in the previous era and regionalism was the next visitor who'd come to stay. European rugby came with it and, before the end of this era, the door was closed on that old familiar home, Stradey. The end of a long and rich relationship during which the club won nearly eighty per cent of all games they played on that hallowed turf. Truly a place they called home.

Author Jon Gower says about his home town that Llanelli is the same as any other. Only different. And so too with that town's sporting religion. It might now be different, but it still remained the same. The heritage was still there, the players continued to be developed, the fans turned up to cheer their Scarlet heroes.

2001 saw the introduction of the Celtic League, nine Welsh teams alongside our Celtic cousins who were now invited to the table as well. Four Irish and two Scottish teams joined the Welsh in a league which was heavily criticised by the leaders of the game in England as being second rate. Comments that actually flew in the face of statistics in the end. But no sooner had this baby league reached the terrible twos than things changed again. Enter Regional Rugby in Wales.

There had been much talk of reorganising Welsh rugby. Many different permutations were put together until eventually everyone settled on one that could work. There would be five regions in Wales which should ensure a higher standard of competition, a higher standard of player and, therefore, improve the national team. Llanelli managed to avoid all attempts to merge it with, yes, Swansea for goodness sake! It was to stand alone, representing the West and the North of Wales.

The new system was introduced in the 2003-2004 season, which was to prove a good one for Llanelli. They won the Celtic League title, four points ahead of Ulster and the Newport Gwent Dragons. Outside-half Gareth Bowen was third top points scorer for the season, behind Neil Jenkins and Gavin Henson. As the regions became top-flight professional teams, a new tier of rugby was formed for the semi-professional players. In Llanelli, this was the team which was to carry the Llanelli RFC name forward, with the region adopting the nick-name which had been chanted on the terraces for decades.

'I knew that I had arrived at a club with something more to it than the ordinary.' Simon Easterby.

These changes meant the end of such long established rivalries between Llanelli and Neath, Aberavon, Pontypridd, Pontypool and all the traditional clubs hewn from coal and forged in steel, although Llanelli RFC, the semi-professional team, proudly continues this tradition. Welsh first class games were now played between Cardiff Blues, Newport Gwent Dragons, the Ospreys, the Celtic Warriors and the Llanelli Scarlets. It was a move that took the club back to the kind of fixture list it enjoyed in its very first years, playing only a handful of Welsh teams.

Quinnell and Botica

So much for the changes. What of things that stayed the same? The overwhelming success of the 1992 -1993 season had given the club a definite impetus. Gareth Jenkins and Alan Lewis kept on keeping on, building on their success. Stars were still being made and one player who came to dominate throughout the early years of this era was the colossus Scott Quinnell. He was already a hit at Stradey, but his try against France at Cardiff in 1994 as a twenty-one year old drew him to the attention of the wider rugby world. Scott's contribution to Llanelli rugby is immense, as is the contribution of the Quinnell family – father Derek and his sons, Scott, Craig and Gavin.

Scott played for the club twice, sandwiched between visits to Wigan and Richmond, making 179 appearances for his home team and scoring 69 tries.

A new, professional era called for a new type of rugby star. Llanelli got into this market very early on and the star duly arrived in the form of Frano Botica – very much a flagship signing of the football type. He played his first game for Llanelli on 1st October 1996. He gave his all on the pitch and contributed significantly to nurturing a certain youngster called Stephen Jones. He contributed the points on the pitch too – 450 points in 42 games.

But as popular as he was, and as much as he contributed to the club on and off the pitch, his arrival at the club wasn't the best business news for Llanelli. The cost of bringing him in proved too much. For that, and for other reasons, significant debts accrued and the club found themselves having to sell Stradey to the WRU for £1.25million in order to survive. A rescue package was drawn up involving a group of fans and significant backing from a few individuals.

Many choose to remember only these black days of debt. A more appropriate response would be to salute the fervor, enthusiasm and dedication of those who put their money where their mouths were and turned the club around. Stradey was soon back in Llanelli hands and success followed on the pitch as well. The passion of the Scarlets faithful is often mentioned worldwide – well, in 1996-1997 it was put through the fire and it came out the other side, strengthened and renewed.

Another man came to Llanelli from across Offa's Dyke at about the same time too. Simon Easterby, who came from the Leeds Tykes having been signed for them by ex-Llanelli and Wales stalwart, Phil Davies. Simon was more than aware of the Llanelli heritage before arriving, but he says he remembers exactly when he experienced that legacy for the first time:

I remember exactly when that sense of a legacy began to kick-in for me. It was the 2000 Welsh Cup final against Swansea in the brand new Millennium Stadium, Cardiff. Llanelli had an amazing record in Welsh Cup competitions. In 1999 the Wales international centre, Scott Gibbs, had stirred things up between the two finalists, saying that when the two teams had met in that year's final and Swansea had won 37-10, it had been a case of 'men against boys'! He still stood by his words when challenged to withdraw them. So, it was 'game on' in 2000! We carried that niggle into the final. The word revenge is often used, and we needed no more motivation than Scott's words! And that, despite having the greatest rugby motivator, Gareth Jenkins, as our coach. We won the 2000 final 22-12 and the Cup was ours once more.

I knew then that I had arrived at a club with something more to it than the norm.

Along with Simon, into the squad which was developing at the end of the Nineties, came Stephen Jones, and these two would go on to influence the club significantly for years to come. Mark Jones pitched up at around the same time and all three went on to play significant coaching roles at the Scarlets. Also arriving at Stradey was a young seventeen-year-old Dafydd Jones and, a little after him, Dwayne Peel. Dwayne went on to be a British Lion and Wales' most capped scrum-half, until he lost that record to another player groomed by Llanelli, Mike Phillips. Fresh faced Daf Jones played over 200 games for the Scarlets and won 42 caps for his country. He remembers the impact of walking in to the Stradey dressing room for the first time:

A massive part of the thrill for me was the fact that Wayne Proctor, Rupert Moon, Nigel Davies and Tony Copsey were there. They had played for the Scarlets in their victory against world

In 1992, the Scarlets' favourite North Walian, hooker Robin McBryde won Wales Strongest Man competition. His last international appearance for Wales was the game in which they clinched the grand slam in 2005.

When the young Dafydd Jones signed his first dual contract — with Llanelli and Llandovery — it was worth £10,000, with a Ford Mondeo thrown in as well.

15 January 2000 was legendary BBC TV commentator Bill McLaren's one and only visit to Stradey. He commented for Grandstand on Llanelli v Wasps in the Heineken Cup. Llanelli won.

Top: The last squad at the Scarlets' last full season at Stradey. Above: Try machine Garan Evans scored 125 tries for his club. He's now the team manager.

2014-2015 Squad. Back row (l-r): Frazier Climo, Michael Tagicakibau, Steffan Hughes, Peter Edwards, Wyn Jones, Kyle Evans, Rhodri Jones, Daniel Jones, Rhodri Davies, Steffan Evans, Will Boyde.

Top middle row (l-r): Steven Shingler, Kristian Phillips, Rory Pitman, Craig Price, Richard Kelly, Aaron Shingler, Jake Ball, Johan Snyman, Lewis Rawlins, Phil Day, Sion Bennett, Josh Lewis.

Bottom middle row (l-r) Rhodri Williams, Adam Warren, Harry Robinson, Aled Davies, Rob Evans, James Davies, Darran Harries, Samson Lee, Ben Leung, Gareth Owen, Jordan Williams, Jacobie Adriaanse, Connor Lloyd, Aaron Warren.

Front row (l-r): Gareth Davies, Rhys Priestland, Phil John, John Barclay, Liam Williams, Scott Williams (vc), Ken Owens (c), Rob McCusker, Emyr Phillips, Regan King, George Earle, Kirby Myhill.

champions Australia in '92/'93, a game that I saw as a boy and which fired my enthusiasm for rugby and for Llanelli RFC. Now I was in the same dressing room as them!

Also new at the club in the last years of the Nineties, was Vernon Cooper, a forward who played over 300 times for Llanelli and who later became involved coaching Llanelli RFC semi-pro team (2008-2012). Slightly longer established, having made his debut against Bath in 1993, was Garan Evans, scorer of 125 tries on the wing and now Scarlets team manager. He was joined in 1994 by hooker Robin McBryde – another who went on to play an active coaching role at the club and is now the Wales forwards coach. When Robin finished playing, Matthew Rees was already in place at Llanelli, having moved there when the Celtic Warriors region disbanded. He captained the club, captained Wales and is a British Lion.

Llanelli certainly has an honourable tradition of keeping its stars, and those stars have a knack of not wanting to leave the club but continuing to serve it long after their boots are hanging on the hook.

Saints and Sospans

Another innovation during these years was the spectre of European competition rugby. Llanelli have been in so many memorable games played under the banner of European cup rugby. However, top of the tree have to be the epic battles against Northampton.

It was the year of the Millennium. The showdown was at the Madejski Stadium, Reading. It was the semi-final of the Heineken Cup and, in a game that was to be called a superb advertisement for Northern Hemisphere rugby, Scarlets narrowly lost to the Saints, 38-21 in a game which featured a last minute 50 yard penalty from Paul Grayson.

When 2003-2004 arrived, Llanelli and Northampton found themselves pitched against each other again, this time in the group stages. Llanelli beat them in the first leg at Stradey, 14 -9, thanks to a Scott Quinnell try and three penalties from Stephen Jones. No one expected a Llanelli win in the return fixture at Franklin Gardens – former England international and now Sky pundit Stuart Barnes, particularly so. He pointed out Llanelli's lack of bottle in previous encounters and coach Gareth Jenkins was incensed! The result? Northampton 9 Scarlets 18. They were in the quarter final and Northampton were out. Apart from the win, the highlight was 'that Barry Davies try.' Picking up a ball that was lower than his laces the fullback raced ahead in one movement and carried on to the try-line as if there was no one in front of him.

An away victory against Toulouse in 2006 is another European highlight. In a nine-try thriller

Above: Morgan Stoddart.
Below: The modern art of the lineout as demonstrated by the high-and-lifted-up Dafydd Jones and his fellow forwards.

in Stade Ernest Wallon, Scarlets beat the French giants 41 points to 34! Llanelli scored five of those tries and Stephen Jones kicked the rest of the points – five conversions and two penalties. What a return for him to the Scarlets fold, having played for the previous two seasons in France with Clermont Auvergne. With typical understated enthusiasm, coach Phil Davies summed-up this epic encounter in this way:

I thought if we put something together in the second half we'd have a chance of achieving something and fortunately we've achieved something quite special.

The club today

The club today is more complex in its structure than it's ever been. When regionalisation came in, a new team was formed, Llanelli RFC. That's hard to get your head around! But the semi-professional team that is branded as Llaneli RFC now, is actually the new creation. The nickname that's over a century old, the Scarlets, is now the official name of what was referred to previously as Llanelli RFC. That's as detailed as a book like this needs to get. Llanelli RFC have enjoyed successes since representing the town in the semi-pro, in particular, maintaining the cup successes previously enjoyed by the club.

Under the professional and the semi-professional umbrellas, is a structure created to develop rugby in every possible way. The Academy is a particular success, acting as the bridge between the traditional feeder clubs in the surrounding area and the professional and semi-professional game. Since 2007 – 2008, 62 players have graduated from the Academy, 19 to sign semi-pro contracts and 43 to sign professional ones. In the Rugby World Cup this year, 2015, 4 of the Scarlets with the Wales squad came through the Academy – Ken Owens, Scott Williams, Samson Lee and Gareth Davies. Liam Williams came through Llanelli RFC. Also with Wales in the tournament is Northampton's George North, another Scarlets Academy graduate. Nurturing local talent is still a core value a hundred and forty years later. This year sees the 50th anniversary of the Llanelli Youth team.

In many ways, this chapter is still being written. It's possibly the hardest of all to write as so many can remember the years of this era in such detail. We can remember so many more players than those of eras gone by, so many matches, both painful and joyful, so many incidents, both on and off the field. Consequently, our list of who and what should be included here will be significantly longer than any other era we think about. We have yet to gain the sense of perspective that time affords us, and I'm afraid that chapter is for a fan in the future to finish.

The sheer romance of rugby in the rain and mud! One time Scarlet and Wales captain Matthew Rees has seen something he thinks the ref needs to know about.

One way rugby changed following regionalisation
is the increasing use of players from abroad.
Australian David Lyons became a firm favourite
when he chose to move to Llanelli.

The steam room!

The legacy continues – Wales' 2012 Magnificent Six!
Grand Slam winners Ken Owens, Scott Williams,
Rhys Priestland, George North, Matthew Rees and
Jonathan Davies.

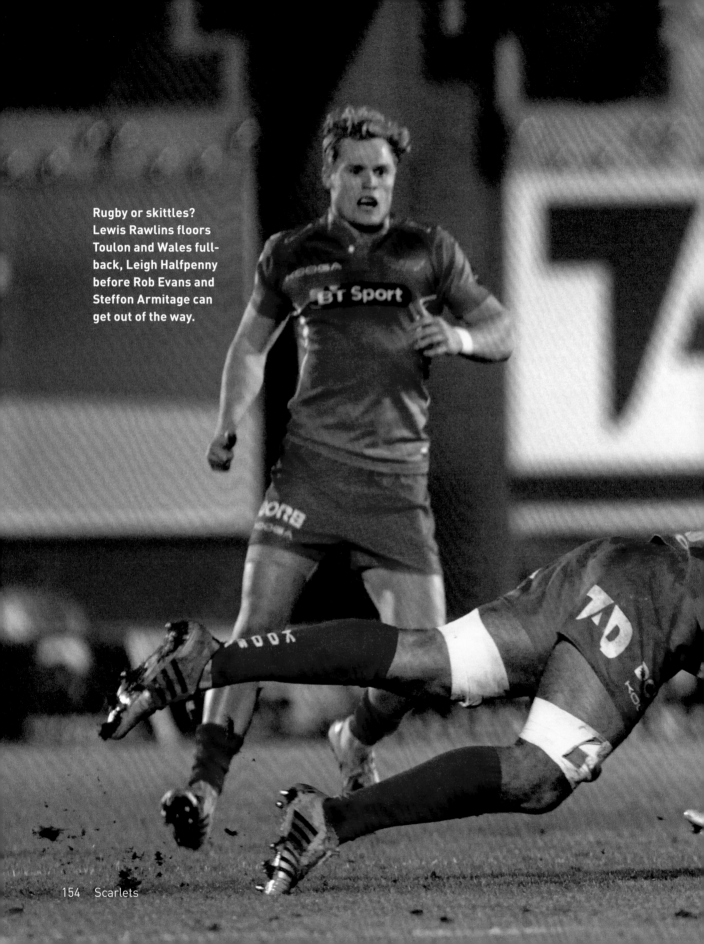

Rugby or skittles? Lewis Rawlins floors Toulon and Wales full-back, Leigh Halfpenny before Rob Evans and Steffon Armitage can get out of the way.

For so many, rugby is an integral part of marking the coming together in marriage, as well as the beginning and the end of life.

Women's rugby has really taken off in the last few years. The Scarlets women's team already enjoying success.

WALES
GRAND SLAM WINNERS
2005

While at Llanelli, George North established so many records in world rugby that he probably holds the record for the most records! When he was 18 years 214 days old he became the youngest player ever to score a try in his debut for Wales; after that, he became the youngest player to

have scored two tries in his debut, with the opposition being a major rugby nation; the youngest player ever to have scored two tries against a major rugby nation, whether on his debut or not; the first player of any age to have scored two tries while making his debut against South Africa. Over 500 players have made their international debut against the Springbok, and 34 of them had scored tries on their debut. But none had scored two tries — until George North.

George North meeting the oldest living Scarlet, Peter Rees, one of the Magnificent Seven of 1947.

The Club has always been seen as the club for the Welsh speaking community, with the Welsh only scoreboard at both stadia being one sign of that.

The terraces of Stradey are known for the banter thrown by fans at players and referees alike, especially the Tanner Bank. One of the classics has to be the words bellowed by one of the town's ministers of religion in the direction of a ref who was having an appalling game. Keen to avoid profanity but frustrated by a particularly shocking decision he shouted at the official, 'Hey ref! Bring your parents to chapel in the morning and I'll marry them!'

'The one thing that stood out on that day was the passion and intensity of the crowd. That hit us hard.'
Bryan Williams, the President of the New Zealand RFU, who played for his country against Llanelli in October 1972, sums up what world rugby thinks of the Scarlets faithful fans.

Stephen Jones
Hero of the era

Without doubt, it has to be Stephen Jones – well, there's no doubt for me at least. And this is for a number of reasons: for his contribution on the pitch; the points he's scored; the way he marshals and controls games in a style that's the opposite of flamboyant and flash. All of the above. But it's also for the way he nurtures and encourages younger players and the way he carries himself himself as a professional sportsman.

Aberystwyth-born Stephen Michael Jones arrived at Stradey as a pupil at Ysgol Gyfun Bro Myrddin, Carmarthen and played against Maesteg in a midweek away friendly. An inauspicious start to say the least. He had already represented Wales at every age grade and in 1996, a year after his schoolboy appearance for the Scarlets, he was on the books, having chosen not to go to Loughborough University to study for a degree in Biology and Human Movement. He opted for the life of a professional sportsman instead.

The former All Black and rugby league star Frano Botica helped Stephen a lot in the early days, taking the youngster onto the Stradey pitch time and time again to practice kicking at goal. But soon Stephen was first choice number ten, going on to play over two hundred games during two spells at Llanelli and scoring 2850 points, becoming the club's all time top scorer.

His first period with Llanelli began in 1996 and lasted until the end of the 2003-2004 season when he went to the Massif Central of France to join Clermont in a move indicative of rugby's new direction. Professionalism meant transfers, and increasingly, as the professional game developed, they were big money transfers. In Stephen's second year at Clermont he was chosen by French journalists as the outside-half of the season. Yet, after two years in France, Stephen came back and rejoined Llanelli at the start of the 2006-2007 season. The story of that season has already been told – the team reaching the semi-final of the Heineken Cup. What has yet to be mentioned is that Stephen was only the third player to reach a total of 500 points in that competition.

Stephen's international career got off to the same inauspicious start as his club career. He had his first cap when he came on as a replacement in that fateful game in 1998 when South Africa trounced Wales 96-13 (Llanelli try machine Garan Evans also had his first cap in that game). Stephen went on from that to show enough form to be considered for the Welsh World Cup squad in 1999. He subsequently won 104 caps for Wales, 86 of them as starts, the rest as a replacement. Cap 103 came against France in that infamous World Cup semi-final in 2011 and cap 104 was in the third place play-off in the same competition, when Wales lost to Australia.

He scored 917 points for his country in total, scoring 7 of Wales' 18 points in their 21-18 loss to Australia in 2011, his last game for his country. He was a also major influence on Wales' Grand Slam win in 2005, with many saying that the Six Nations campaign saw Jones playing at his very best. He contributed 44 points in the 2009 Six Nations campaign, another Grand Slam year.

Back with the Scarlets. The 2015-2016 season sees the return of Stephen Jones as the backs coach.

The British Lions soon came calling and he first toured with them off the back of Wales' Grand Slam of 2005. That year the Lions went to New Zealand, and Stephen was one of four outside-halves chosen by Sir Clive Woodward. In 2009, he was chosen for the Lions tour of South Africa where he started all three Tests. He most certainly made his mark in the second Test though, for although the Lions lost 28-25, Stephen was on top form. He scored one conversion out of one, five penalties out of five and one drop goal out of just one attempted. This twenty point haul broke the Lions record for points in a Test against South Africa.

We'll leave it to Gareth Jenkins, the coach who probably knows him better than most, to sum up Stephen Jones.

[Stephen] has the respect and regard of his players, leadership qualities that are evident for all to see and the talent and ability to lead from the front at game time.

Some years into adult life, powerhouse Scott Quinnell learned that he was dyslexic. Since then he has campaigned tirelessly to improve the resources and education for people with similar learning difficulties. He once joked that as dyslexia significantly affected his co-ordination, that's why he used to keep hold of the ball and run so much. 'If I didn't have dyslexia', he quipped, 'I probably would have passed the ball more!'

Scarlet half-back partnership Stephen Jones and Dwayne Peel are also business partners in the food industry. They are part of the set-up that saw the opening of Sosban Restaurant in Llanelli, which has since been voted the best in Wales. They have both been known to put on their whites and learn the skills of the kitchen, but have asked for any photographic evidence of this to be destroyed!

Left: The pride and the passion, as shown
by Rhys Priestland and team mates.
Top: Celebrating being the 2003-2004 Celtic
League Champions, winning 16 out of 22
games and scoring 57 tries. Right: Actor Julian
Lewis Jones in Hollywood for the premier of
a film he was in, *Invictus*, wearing Scarlet!

Rhys Thomas, a modern day prop, on the charge.

Nigel Davies. A player for Trimsaran RFC, Llanelli RFC and Wales, Head Coach at Llanelli and part of the Welsh coaching set up in the 2000s.

LLANELLi
SCARLETS

Scott Williams' epic Triple Crown winning try
for Wales at Twickenham in 2012 captured
on canvas by young artist Elin Sian.

So it was goodbye Stradey... and hello Parc y Scarlets. Right: Jon Davies had the honour of scoring the first ever try in the new stadium, in a game against the Cardiff Blues.

Parc y Scarlets
Sospans still on the posts!

Much has been said about the grand old lady that was Stradey Park, a venue, a home and a fortress that is, of course, by no means forgotten. She will, I am sure, be cherished, sung about and remembered for many a long year to come. But there is now a new home of the Scarlets in Llanelli. In 2008 the club took another pioneering step in the spirit of their predecessors who developed Stradey in 1879, 1904 and in the 1950s. A purpose build stand-alone rugby stadium was opened at the other end of town to Stradey. There was to be no

ground sharing with a football team here, as is the trend throughout the UK. Parc y Scarlets is unique in being a rugby-only new build stadium.

The role the passionate fans play in the life of the club has been shown already. This was also the case in the move to Parc y Scarlets, even to the point of influencing the design of the stadium. Again, contrary to other new build stadia of this era, it is not an all seated ground. There is a terraced area in front of the northern stand, the result of a specific request from the Supporters Trust. There was a strong desire to replicate, at

27 March 2013. The unveiling ceremony for the statue of Ray Gravell that graces the front aspect of Parc y Scarlets. The sculptor, David Williams-Ellis is behind Grav's left knee, next to Roy Bergiers, former player and club President. Grav's wife Mari and daughters Manon and Gwenan see to the unveiling.

least in part, some of the terraced atmosphere of the Tanner Bank, the Pwll End, the Enclosure and the Scoreboard end at Stradey. Nearly two thousand Scarlet bannered and scarved fans can pack in to this standing area.

The link with the club's heritage can be seen in so many other places too. Four giant figures from the Scarlet past lend their names to the main hospitality areas in the stadium. Carwyn James and Phil Bennett have lounges named after them on the third floor, where the main partners and sponsors meet in the shadow of the Maestro Carwyn James while Phil Bennett welcomes the patrons. Another lounge, the one used by the Business Club, carries the family name of the many Quinnells who have pulled on the Scarlet jersey. Other hospitality boxes bear the names of 15 former greats associated with the club: Ray Williams, Andy Hill, Albert Jenkins, Ieuan Evans, Norman Gale,

Phil Davies, Phil May, R. H. Williams, Gareth Jenkins, Marlston Morgan, Ivor Jones, Huw Evans/Stuart Gallacher, Rupert Moon, Charles William Mansel-Lewis.

Standing alone alongside the stadium is the Dutch barn structure that lends itself to indoor training, the Canolfan Delme Thomas Centre. It has a full size pitch within its walls, again a unique feature, and on match days it is the focus for pre-match fun – hog roasts and entertainment for supporters of all ages. On non-match days it is regularly used by local groups, schools and other organisations.

Left top and bottom: After nearly a century, home is a different place. The man behind that move, then Chief Executive Stuart Gallagher, contemplates the old as the new is being built. Above: All unpacked at the new home – who'd be a kit man?

Parc y Scarlets in all its glory. The place where new legends will be made.

Schoolboys and girls who play for their village or local teams enjoy the privilege of being a guard of honour as they eagerly await their heroes.

Cochyn the club mascot. Cheerleader and rabble-rouser extraordinaire!

Brand new stadium, state of the art pitch, a hundred year old nickname on one stand and Grav's favourite catch-phrase on the other.

As with all good designs, the structure reflects the heart and the soul of the organisation it houses. Nowhere is this seen more clearly than in the naming process.

The various areas of Parc y Scarlets reflect the links with the community, the one central thread running through the Scarlet story from day one, like a shaft of local steel. Another thread is visible in the choices of names too, a thread that strengthens as each decade gives way to the next – the thread of heritage. In addition, the fact that, so far, the club have not sold the naming rights for the stadium itself emphasises further the felt need for a strong and clear identity. Two of the men whose names can be seen on the stadium walls emphasised these points when the new stadium opened.

It's important that we retain powerful links to our great traditions. The club's had great players and great administrators and it's important that we don't forget that.
Derek Quinnell.

This is a ground all about the rugby and the people. We're traditionally a working class town and the supporters have been wonderful over the years. The name gives them an identity.
Phil Bennett.

Sometimes it's even as if the spirit of the past is determined to guide the club forward, even without the club itself being aware of the influence it exerts. It turns out that the brand new, state-of-the-art stadium on a brand new site isn't that brand new after all. Parc y Scarlets was built almost exactly on the same spot as a sporting stadium which was built in 1894 when the rugby club was less than twenty years old. The County Athletic Ground stood where the Pemberton Retail park is today, its back end overlapping the present Parc y Scarlets. It was predominantly built for another

popular sporting pastime, cycling races, and the Llanelly Wheelers, the town's cycling club, were one of the County Athletic's backers.

This was also the first home of Llanelli football team. Men from Stoke had come down to pass on their knowledge of the pottery craft and industry to local pottery workers and they couldn't cope with the game they saw played in Llanelli, the one with a funny shaped ball. They joined locals of the same persuasion, football took hold and they turned to the Athletic for a home. Galloway races were a popular draw there too – the racing of Galloway horses. And boxing events drew thousands, certainly when Llanelli-born champion boxer William 'Gipsy' Daniels fought there. He was the Light Heavyweight champion of Britain. Unfortunately there's no record of him saying whether he preferred to box in the County Athletic or in Madison Square Garden, New York where he fought twice! And just to round off the rugby link, Gipsy's father played rugby for Llanelli.

As usually happens with the construction of new facilities, other complimentary businesses also develop in their wake. Those coming to The County Athletic Ground needed somewhere to eat, drink and stay – arise The Halfway Hotel, which is still standing and now meeting the needs of Parc y Scarlets fans. A Travelodge and Beefeater have likewise been built to appeal to the Parc y Scarlets faithful and visitors alike.

A sign of the times when the County Athletic opened was the boycott of the opening event by many of the town's religious leaders. Not only was there opposition to the fact that boxing would be held there – echoing the disdain that many felt when the brutal game of rugby started in the town – but the opening ceremony was arranged for Easter Monday. That was too much for many, and they stayed away. Many older people in the town can remember playing as children on the parts of the ground that were still there in the 1930s.

So as we can see, history certainly does repeat itself. People react similarly to changing situations, opportunities become realised in similar ways. There is one very big difference here though. Parc y Scarlets cost £23 million to build, the County Athletic £300!

Today, Parc y Scarlets takes its place in the wider sporting and leisure provision of Carmarthenshire. The Local Authority are partners in the running of the Stadium as they are in the Jack Nicklaus designed golf course at Machynys, the Ffos Las Racecourse at Carway and the Pembrey Race Circuit.

In Llanelli town, as in Llanelli rugby, there's no escaping history. It's both where we've come from and how we got to where we are. And that, of course, is true for everything and everywhere, not just rugby and not just Llanelli. But what differs in Llanelli is that there is an acute awareness of the history, and in particular the social and communal history, from which we are forged. It's real. It informs

Left: The Delme Thomas Center, affectionately known as 'the barn', is the place to be on match day for Scarlets fans of all ages.
Top: When it's not match day and when there's no training, it's a home for trade exhibitions and conferences. Above: A fans favourite, the hog roast.

decisions made today both on and off the pitch. The club have long since adopted a refrain from one of the most popular Welsh language songs ever. Renowned folk singer Dafydd Iwan penned Yma O Hyd (We're Still Here) to show fortitude in the light of opposition and oppression. A clip from the chorus of that song has been played when Llanelli, or the Llanelli Scarlets, or the Scarlets, have scored a try since the Stradey days.

Ry'n ni yma o hyd,
Ry'n ni yma o hyd,
Er gwaetha pawb a phopeth,
Er gwaetha pawb a phopeth
Ry'n ni yma o hyd.
Ry'n ni yma o hyd,

We're still here. We're still here
Despite everyone and everything
Despite everyone and everything
We're still here.
We're still here

These are words which aren't sung in the spirit of mawkish sentiment or chocolate box nostalgia. They're not words read through Scarlet-tinted spectacles. Instead they're sung with the same spirit of defiance and unity which has seen the Scarlets story survive a hundred and forty years both at the centre of world club rugby and at the centre of people's lives in the West Wales town of Llanelli. We're still here, and we're looking forward to the next 140 years.

Heritage Trail

Top right: Another historical milestone passed – the club's 5000th game on 23 September 2011. A handful of the stars who've signed the Memorial Wall: Garan Evans, Terry Davies, Peter Rees, Rupert Moon, Handel Greville and Ieuan Evans.

Right: Events at Parc y Scarlets draw big names from TV and film. Here it's actor Ricky Tomlinson, from Royle Family fame – and he's proud to wear Scarlet! **Far right:** BBC News anchor and Llanelli boy, Huw Edwards, opening the Heritage Trail.

Left: Side by side with burgers and pints, the concourse is home to the Scarlets Heritage Trail, telling yesterday's story today.

Where the next chapters will be written...

Internationals and Lions

Scarlets Internationals

The following Scarlets players have represented their countries at international level (Wales unless otherwise stated):

	Name	First cap vs	Year
1	Harry Bowen	England	1881
2	Alfred Cattell	England	1882
3	Fred L. Margrave	England	1884
4	William B. Roderick	Ireland	1884
5	Evan Roberts	England	1886
6	John G. Lewis	Ireland	1887
7	E. J. (Ned) Roberts	Scotland	1888
8	Dan Griffiths	Maoris	1888
9	Gitto Griffiths	Ireland	1889
10	Tom Morgan	Ireland	1889
11	Percy Lloyd	Scotland	1890
12	Stephen Thomas	Scotland	1890
13	D. J. Daniel	Scotland	1891
14	C. B. Nicholl	Ireland	1891
15	R. L. Thomas	Scotland	1891
16	W. H. Thomas	Scotland	1891
17	J. Conway Rees	Scotland	1892
18	D. W. Nicholl	Ireland	1894
19	Owen Badger	England	1895
20	Ben Davies	England	1895
21	Evan Lloyd	Scotland	1895
22	Dai Morgan	Ireland	1895
23	Cliff Bowen	England	1896
24	Jack Evans	Scotland	1896
25	Bill Morris	Scotland	1896
26	R. T. Gabe	Ireland	1901
27	John Strand-Jones	England	1902
28	Danny Walters	England	1902
29	Willie Arnold	Scotland	1903
30	Harry Watkins	Scotland	1904
31	Tom Evans	Ireland	1906
32	Bailey Davies	England	1907
33	Jim Watts	England	1907
34	Harold Thomas	France	1912
35	Jack Morgan	South Africa	1912
36	Rev. Alban Davies	England	1914
37	Ivor T. Davies	Scotland	1914
38	W. J. Watts	England	1914
39	Ike Fowler	N Z Army	1919
40	Gwyn Francis	N Z Army	1919
41	W. T. Harvard	N Z Army	1919
42	Bryn S. Evans	England	1920
43	Albert Jenkins	England	1920
44	Edgar Morgan	Ireland	1920
45	Bryn Williams	Scotland	1920
46	Graham Davies	France	1921
47	Frank Evans	Scotland	1921
48	J. G. Stephens	England	1922
49	Gethin Thomas	England	1923
50	Dai John	France	1923
51	Ivor E. Jones	England	1924
52	J. Elwyn Evans	Scotland	1924
53	Cliff Williams	New Zealand	1924
54	W. J. Jones	Ireland	1924
55	Ernie Finch	France	1924
56	W. Idris Jones	England	1925
57	Will Lewis	France	1925
58	Arthur John	Ireland	1925
59	J. D. Bartlett	Scotland	1927
60	Iorwerth Jones	NSW	1927
61	Watcyn Thomas	England	1927
62	Archie Skym	England	1927
63	Edgar Jones	France	1930
64	Jim Lang	France	1931
65	Bryn Evans	England	1933
66	Bryn Howells	England	1934
67	Bert Jones	Scotland	1934
68	Harry Truman	England	1934
69	W. H. 'Bill' Clement	England	1937
70	Emrys Evans	England	1937
71	F. L. Morgan	England	1938

72	Elvet Jones	Scotland	1939
73	Howard Davies	England	1947
74	Stan Williams	England	1947
75	Griff Bevan	England	1947
76	Peter Rees	France	1947
77	Les Williams	England	1947
78	Ossie Williams	England	1947
79	Handel Greville	Australia	1947
80	Des Jones	England	1948
81	Peter Stone	France	1949
82	Peter Evans	England	1951
83	Gerwyn Williams	England	1951
84	Lewis Jones	South Africa	1951
85	Denzil Thomas	Ireland	1954
86	R. H. Williams	Ireland	1954
87	Len Davies	France	1954
88	Ray Williams	Scotland	1954
89	Ian Macgregor	Scotland	1955
90	Alun Thomas	Scotland	1955
91	Terry Davies	England	1957
92	Geoff Howells	England	1957
93	Cyril Davies	Ireland	1957
94	Henry Morgan	Ireland	1957
95	Wynne Evans	Australia	1958
96	Carwyn James	Australia	1958
97	Onllwyn Brace	Scotland	1960
98	Denis Evans	South Africa	1960
99	D. Ken Jones	England	1962
100	Robert Morgan	England	1962
101	Brian Davies	Ireland	1962
102	John Warlow	Ireland	1962
103	Norman Gale	England	1963
104	Terry Price	England	1965
105	Barry John	Australia	1966
106	Delme Thomas	Australia	1966
107	Phil Bennett	France	1969
108	Stuart Gallacher	France	1970
109	Roy Mathias	France	1970
110	Barry Llewelyn	England	1971
111	Roy Bergiers	England	1972
112	Derek Quinnell	France	1972
113	Tom David	France	1973
114	J. J. Williams	France	1973
115	Ray Gravell	France	1975
116	Paul Ringer	Ireland	1979

117	Clive Griffiths	England	1979
118	Peter Morgan	Scotland	1980
119	David Nicholas	England	1981
120	David Pickering	England	1983
121	Mark Douglas	Scotland	1984
122	Phil Lewis	Australia	1984
123	Alun Davies	Australia	1984
124	Phil Davies	England	1985
125	Ieuan Evans	France	1987
126	Anthony Buchanan	Tonga	1987
127	Phil May	England	1988
128	Jonathan Davies	England	1988
129	Jonathan Griffiths	New Zealand	1988
130	Nigel Davies	New Zealand	1988
131	Gary Jones	New Zealand	1988
132	Carwyn Davies	W. Samoa	1988
133	Laurance Delaney	Ireland	1989
134	Mark Perego	Scotland	1990
135	Emyr Lewis	Ireland	1991
136	Luc Evans	France	1991
137	Colin Stephens	Ireland	1992
138	Anthony Copsey	Ireland	1992
139	Wayne Proctor	Australia	1992
140	Ricky Evans	England	1993
141	Rupert Moon	France	1993
142	Andrew Lamerton	France	1993
143	Neil Boobyer	Zimbabwe	1993
144	Lyn Jones	Zimbabwe	1993
145	Scott Quinnell	Canada	1993
146	H. Williams-Jones	Fiji	1994
147	Robin Mcbryde	South Africa	1995
148	Spencer John	Scotland	1995
149	Justin Thomas	South Africa	1995
150	Craig Quinnell	Fiji	1995
151	Matthew Wintle	Italy	1996
152	Gwyn Jones	Italy	1996
153	Mike Voyle	France	1996
154	Frano Botica (For Croatia)	Latvia	1997
155	Andrew Gibbs	USA	1997
156	Chris Wyatt	Zimbabwe	1998
157	Garan Evans	South Africa	1998
158	Darril Williams	South Africa	1998
159	Stephen Jones	South Africa	1998

160	Salesi Finau (For Tonga)	Georgia	1999
161	David Hodges (For USA)	England	1999
162	Dafydd James	France	1999
163	S. (Jonny) Koloi (For Tonga)	New Zealand	1999
164	Simon Easterby (For Ireland)	Scotland	2000
165	Matt Cardey	Scotland	2000
166	Mark Jones	England	2000
167	Guy Easterby (For Ireland)	Romania	2001
168	Dwayne Peel	Japan	2001
169	Leigh Davies	Ireland	2001
170	Luke Gross (For USA)	South Africa	2001
171	Iestyn Thomas	South Africa	2002
172	Martyn Madden	South Africa	2002
173	Jamie Cudmore (For Canada)	USA	2002
174	Dafydd Jones	Fiji	2002
175	Vernon Cooper	Canada	2002
176	Matthew Watkins	Italy	2003
177	Mark Taylor	Australia	2003
178	Mike Phillips	Romania	2003
179	John Thiel (For Canada)	France	2004
180	Matthew Rees	USA	2005
181	Mike Hercus (For USA)	Wales	2005
182	Tal Selley	USA	2005
183	Alix Popham	Canada	2005
184	Lee Byrne	New Zealand	2005
185	Inoke Afeaki (For Tonga)	Italy	2005
186	Adam M. Jones	England	2006
187	Barry Davies	Ireland	2006
188	Gavin Thomas	Argentina	2006
189	Scott Macleod (For Scotland)	South Africa	2006
190	Gavin Evans	Pacific Islands	2006
191	Morgan Stoddart	South Africa	2007
192	M. Schwalgar (For South Africa)	Fiji	2008
193	Martin Roberts	Canada	2008
194	Jonathan Davies	Canada	2009
195	Daniel Evans	Canada	2009
196	Sean Lamont (For Scotland)	England	2009
197	Deacon Manu (For Fiji)	Scotland	2009
198	Rob McCusker	South Africa	2010
199	Tavis Knoyle	New Zealand	2010
200	George North	South Africa	2010
201	Josh Turnbull	Scotland	2011
202	Rhys Priestland	Scotland	2011
203	Scott Williams	Barbarians	2011
204	Sione Timani (For Tonga)	USA	2011
205	Ken Owens	Namibia	2011
206	Ben Morgan (For England)	Scotland	2012
207	Aaron Shingler	Scotland	2012
208	Lou Reed	Scotland	2012
209	Rhodri Jones	Barbarians	2012
210	Liam Williams	Barbarians	2012
211	Adam Warren	Barbarians	2012
212	Viliame Iongi (For Tonga)	USA	2012
213	Tomas Vallejos Cinalli (For Argentina)	Georgia	2012
214	Emyr Phillips	Japan	2013
215	Horatiu Pungea (For Romania)	Tonga	2013
216	John Barclay (For Scotland)	Japan	2013
217	Samson Lee	Argentina	2013
218	Rhodri Williams	Tonga	2013
219	Gareth Davies	South Africa	2014
220	Jake Ball	Ireland	2014
221	Rob Evans	Ireland	2015
222	D. T. H. Van Der Merwe (For Canada)	Japan	2015

Scarlets Lions

Scarlets players who have had the honour of playing for the British & Irish Lions.

1	Ivor Jones	1930
2	Elvet Jones	1938
3	W. H. Clement	1938
4	Lewis Jones	1950
5	Alun Thomas	1955
6	R. H. Williams	1955, 1959
7	Terry Davies	1959
8	Ken Jones	1962
9	Delme Thomas	1966, 1968, 1971
10	Terry Price	1966
11	Derek Quinnell	1971, 1977, 1980
12	Phil Bennett	1974, 1977 (Captain)
13	Roy Bergiers	1974
14	Tom David	1974
15	J. J. Williams	1974, 1977
16	Ray Gravell	1980
17	Peter Morgan	1980
18	Ieuan Evans	1989, 1993, 1997
19	Scott Quinnell	2001
20	Robin Mcbryde	2001
21	Dwayne Peel	2005
22	Simon Easterby	2005
23	Stephen Jones	2009
24	Matthew Rees	2009
25	Jonathan Davies	2013
26	George North	2013

Two Llanelli men have coached the Lions:

Carwyn James	1971
Gareth Jenkins	2005

Carwyn James 1971

Gareth Jenkins 2005

Acknowledgments

It takes a lot of people to put something like this together. My thanks to Darran Phillips, Nia Lloyd and Nerys Jones at The Scarlets; to Caru James and the staff at Llanelli Public Library; to David Rogers for the freedom to use the rare unseen archive of his grandfather's, former Club Chairman Handel Rogers; to Ian Williams for his contribution to the photographic record of this story and also to Huw Evans, Emyr Young, Steve Pope, Phil Shepard-Lewis, Terry Morris for the same; to Terry Davies, former Scarlet, Welsh international and Lion for stories and photos.

To the Books Council of Wales for their backing; to Graffeg for running with the vision for this book and the high quality of the end product.

A big thank you to Robert Lloyd for reading the manuscript before hand and making many useful suggestions. Thanks also to former Scarlets historian, Les Williams for his contribution. Any mistakes or omissions that remain are mine, not theirs.

And finally to my family – my parents for putting me on the Stradey terraces in the first place and during the last year or so, to Fiona, Lowri, William, Gregory and Dean for every backing and encouragement. Lucky for me, Fiona knows her rugby too!

West is Best!

Scarlets

Parc Y Scarlets, Parc Pemberton,
Llanelli, Sir Gâr SA14 9UZ
www.scarlets.co.uk
comments@scarlets.wales
01554 783900

The Scarlets Supporters Trust – Crys 16

crys16.cymru

Photo credits

© Alan Richards: pages 56-57, 113 (top).
© Alun Gibbard: pages 10, 11, 58 (bottom), 62 (bottom), 93, 94, 102, 103, 108, 109, 110, 113 (bottom), 114, 116, 117, 118, 119, 126, 128, 129, 138, 140, 141, 159.
© Carwyn James Family: pages 89, 91.
© David Jones: page 125.
© David Rogers Collection: pages 54, 55, 72, 73, 74, 75, 76, 77, 78.
© Delme Thomas: pages 86, 87, 97 (left).
© Doug Simpson: page 58 (top).
© E. Meirion Roberts: page 112.
© Elin Sian: page 169.
© Emyr Young: page 185 (bottom left).
© Gesine Thomson: page 167 (bottom).
© Huw Evans Agency: pages 59, 60-61, 63 (top), 134, 135, 146-147.
© Llanelli Library Services: pages 8, 12, 14, 15, 16, 17, 18, 19, 21, 22, 23, 24, 25, 26, 27, 28-29, 30, 31, 32-33, 35, 38, 39, 41, 42, 43, 44, 45, 46, 47, 48, 50, 51, 52, 53, 131.
© Nigel Francis, Principality Weddings and Portraits: page 157 (bottom left).
©Phil Shephard-Lewis: page 101.
©Riley Sports Photography: pages 9, 36-37, 63 (bottom), 121, 123, 139, 143, 148, 149, 150, 151, 152, 153, 154-155, 156, 157 (top and bottom right), 158, 162, 163, 165 (bottom), 166, 168, 170, 171, 172, 173, 174, 175, 185 (top).
© Steve Pope: page 145.
© Terry Davies: pages 68, 115.
© Terry Morris: page 191.
© The Scarlets Collection: pages 49, 62 (top), 65, 66, 67, 69, 70, 79, 81, 82, 83, 84-85, 90, 95, 96, 97 (right), 98-99, 100, 104, 105, 106, 107, 111, 120, 122, 132, 137, 160-161, 165 (top), 167 (top), 176-177, 178-179, 180, 181, 182, 183, 184, 185 (bottom right), 186-187.